Public Education in the South Today and Tomorrow

PUBLIC EDUCATION IN THE SOUTH

TODAY AND TOMORROW

A *Statistical Survey*

EDITED BY
ERNST W. SWANSON AND JOHN A. GRIFFIN

Based on Studies by

JOHN M. MACLACHLAN
TRUMAN M. PIERCE AND ASSOCIATES
ERNST W. SWANSON

Chapel Hill

THE UNIVERSITY OF NORTH CAROLINA PRESS

Copyright, 1955, by
The University of North Carolina Press

Manufactured in the United States of America

Foreword

In the early summer of 1953, when I accepted an assignment from the Fund for the Advancement of Education to direct a study of biracial education in the United States, the project was given urgency by the fact that five public school cases involving segregation were then pending before the Supreme Court. These cases have since been resolved by the historic decision of May 17, 1954, and the implementing decrees handed down a year later.

The new precedent, and the great moral issue upon which it turned, have served to focus attention upon the dual school system in which the great majority of American whites and Negroes have been educated. By its nature, however, the new dispensation also has served to obscure vital aspects of that system—and of the rapidly changing culture and economy which produced it.

The effort to integrate the public schools, and the resistance of many Southerners to the process, makes for controversy and for drama. Yet, despite the profound social implications of the educational patterns now emerging in the region, the studies upon which this volume is based show quite clearly that this is only one of many interrelated changes taking place in the region that extends across a quarter of the nation from Virginia to Texas.

The whole story, I believe, is essentially more dramatic than any of its parts. And, remarkably enough, the drama carries over into the statistical tables that make up the bulk of this work. Here, state by state, are measured the accelerating migration of the Southern people from farm to city, and the great out-migration that still goes on. Here are shown the effects of the industrial revolution, which arrived in the South almost a century after it had begun to transform the rest of the nation. Here are set forth the challenges and the opportunities inherent in the state of flux that now exists everywhere in the region. And here, finally, is a reminder that many of the current problems that seem to loom so large in fact are well on their way to resolution by processes that, because they have come so suddenly, are still little understood.

This volume is in large part based on extension and refinement of material gathered for the Fund's study, and presented in condensed form in *The Negro and the Schools*. Only one who has observed such an undertaking from the inside can appreciate how hard most of these data were to come by, or how much soul-searching was involved in the effort to convert past trends into future projections. My thanks, and those of the Fund, go to all those who labored under pressure on the original research—and to Ernst Swanson and John Griffin, whose tenacity and professional skill brought forth this comprehensive and, I believe, indispensable work.

HARRY S. ASHMORE

Little Rock, Arkansas

Preface

This volume is essentially a handbook on statistics related to the South's educational problem. It started out originally as a general investigation of the problem in its demographic, economic, and sociological dimensions, furthering the research of the Ashmore Project reported by Harry S. Ashmore in *The Negro and the Schools*. John M. Maclachlan, chairman of the Department of Sociology, University of Florida, did the population research; Truman M. Pierce and his associates in the Southern States Cooperative Program in Educational Administration, George Peabody College for Teachers, did the educational research; and Ernst W. Swanson, professor of economics, Emory University, did the economic analysis. John A. Griffin, associate professor of sociology and director of Community Educational Service, Emory University, was administrative coordinator for the project. The products of the separate endeavors became so voluminous that a handbook largely summarizing the abundant statistical material was decided upon.

The editors have sought to treat the educational problem of the South in four facets. These will be described and defined in the first chapter, which summarizes briefly the findings. The eight other chapters are essentially groupings of the most important statistical tables with explanations and interpretations of their contents. The groupings are arrayed to give a statistical sequence to the educational tasks. This sequence runs from the reasons for the problem, to the basic materials upon which its solution must rest, to an evaluation of the South's economic capacity to meet the problem. The final solution in its many details must, of course, be left to the people of the South.

The editors hope that those who read this volume will find themselves better informed on the nature of the South's public education and that the statistics will prove useful in their efforts to cope with the issues involved.

Needless to say, we are indebted to a number of people, to Southern educational leaders, to our colleagues at Emory University, George Peabody College for Teachers, the University of Florida, and to many others. We owe a great debt to Eugene Queen for his statistical work and to Harold C. Fleming for his generous editorial assistance. Our greatest debt is to the Fund for the Advancement of Education which has defrayed the many costs of the research, and particularly to Philip H. Coombs.

Tables 13 through 16, 19, 20, 22 through 29, and 34 through 39 are based upon data which appear in Truman M. Pierce, Bennie E. Carmichael, James B. Kincheloe, R. Edgar Moore, and Galen N. Drewry, *White and Negro Schools in the South: An Analysis of Biracial Education* (copyright, 1955, by Prentice-Hall, Inc., Englewood Cliffs) and are here used with permission of the publisher. Certain population tables are developed from data in the manuscript by John M. Maclachlan and Joe S. Floyd, *This Changing South*.

ERNST W. SWANSON
JOHN A. GRIFFIN

Emory University
May 21, 1955

Contents

Foreword v

Preface vii

Chapter 1. Introduction 3

PART ONE—PUBLIC EDUCATION IN THE SOUTH TODAY

Chapter 2. The People of the South
- The Population of the South... 14
- The Growth of the Southern People.................................... 16
- The Percentage of Negroes in the Population.......................... 18
- The Comparison of the Rates of Increase of White and Negro Population 20
- From Farm to City.. 22
- White and Negro Rates of Urbanization................................ 24
- The Unevenness of Southern Population Growth......................... 26
- The Movement of People in the Southern States........................ 30
- The Exportation of Southern People................................... 32

Chapter 3. The Children of the South
- School-Age Population 34
- School-Age Population by Age Groups.................................. 36
- Enrollment by Race... 38
- Average Daily Attendance... 40
- Enrollment and Attendance by Place of Residence...................... 42

Chapter 4. Some Qualitative Measures of Southern Schooling
- The Median Year of School Completed.................................. 44
- The Pupil Load Per Teacher... 48
- Training Completed by Southern Teachers.............................. 50
- Length of School Term.. 52
- Public School Libraries.. 54
- Vocational Education 56
- Teachers' Salaries 58

Chapter 5. What the South Is Spending for Schooling
- Total School Costs in the South, 1951-52............................. 60
- The Negro's Share of School Dollars.................................. 62
- Total Current Expenditures for Whites and Negroes.................... 64
- Expenditures Per Pupil 66
- City and Country School Dollars...................................... 68
- Instruction Costs as a Percentage of Current Expenditures............ 70
- The Influence of Income and Place of Residence on Expenditures Per Pupil.. 72
- Capital Expenditure Per Pupil.. 74
- Current Expenditures, South and Nation............................... 76

PART TWO—PUBLIC EDUCATION IN THE SOUTH TOMORROW

Chapter 6. Projection of School-Age Population, Enrollment, and Average Daily Attendance
    The 1960 School-Age Population...................................... 80
    The Estimation of School Enrollment Ratios to 1960.................. 82
    Projected 1960 Enrollment... 84
    Ratio of Average Daily Attendance to Enrollment..................... 86
    Average Daily Attendance for 1960................................... 88

Chapter 7. The Price of Equality and Improvement
    Across-the-Board Equalization of Current Expenditures................ 90
    Estimated Capital Deficit as of 1952................................ 92
    The Annual Growth in Current and Transportation Expenditures
        from 1952 to 1960... 94
    Providing Buildings and Equipment for School Population
        Growth to 1960 96

Chapter 8. The Projection of Southern Income
    The Growth of Southern Income....................................... 98
    The Shifting Sources of Income..................................... 100
    Income Projections Under the Conservative Assumption............... 102
    Income Projections Under the Optimistic Assumption................. 104
    A Comparison of the Low and High Income Projections and Their
        Capacity for Meeting Fiscal Needs............................ 106

Chapter 9. The South's Ability to Pay
    Total Costs of Equalization and Improvement and of Providing
        for the Rise in Average Daily Attendance..................... 108
    Projection of Current and Transportation Expenditures,
        1952-53 to 1959-60 110
    Funding and Amortizing the Capital Deficit......................... 112
    Capital Deficits and Their Amortization in the South and by States. 114
    The Growth in Enrollment and the Additional Capital Needs......... 116
    The Fiscal Needs—An Example of Accounting for the Costs........... 118
    Year-by-Year Projection of Total Costs, Current, Transportation,
        and Capital 120
    Comparison of Yearly Total Expenditures with the Yearly High
        and Low Incomes 122

Appendices
    1. The Selection of the Sample...................................... 125
    2. Estimation of White and Negro Current Expenditures, 1951-52..... 126
    3. How Long May It Take the South to Catch Up with the North?..... 126
    4. Methods for Projection of Enrollment............................ 128
    5. Estimation of Capital Deficit................................... 129
    6. Cost Factor for Determining Growth in Capital Requirements...... 130
    7. An Analysis of the Costs of Integration......................... 131
    8. Methods of Income Projection.................................... 132
    9. Estimation of the "Low" Income.................................. 134
    10. Estimation of the "High" Income................................ 136

List of Tables

1. Population of United States, Non-South, South, and Southern States by Decades, 1900-1950 15

2. Percentage Changes in Total Population for United States, Non-South, South, and Southern States by Decades, 1900-1950 17

3. Negro Population as a Percentage of the Total Population for United States, Non-South, South, and Southern States by Decades, 1900-1950.... 19

4. Percentage Change of Population for United States, Non-South, South, and Southern States by Decades by Race, 1900-1950 21

5. Percentage of Total Population Urban or Rural for United States, South, and Southern States by Decades, 1900-1950 23

6. Percentage Change in Urban, Rural Non-Farm, and Rural Farm Population for United States, Non-South, South, and Southern States by Race, 1940-1950 25

7. Population by Counties Increasing and Counties Decreasing and Percentage Change for South and Southern States, 1940-1950 27

8. Distribution of Counties Showing Population Increases and Decreases by Percentage Changes for United States, Non-South, South, and Southern States, 1940-1950 29

9. Natives of South and Southern States Living in Non-Southern States by Race, 1950 31

10. Effect of Cumulative Interstate Migration to 1950 by Percentage Distribution of Native Population, United States, Non-South, South, and Southern States, and Percentage Distribution of Non-Natives Living in South and Southern States by Place of Birth 33

11. School-Age Population as a Percentage of Total Population and Attendance and Enrollment as a Percentage of School-Age Population for the South by Race, 1900-1950 35

12. School-Age Population by Age Groups, 5-13, 14-17, in South and Southern States by Race, 1950 37

13. Elementary and Secondary Enrollment and Percentage Change in South and Southern States by Race, 1939-40 to 1951-52 39

14. Average Daily Attendance in Public Schools of South and Southern States by Race, 1939-40 and 1951-52 41

15. Attendance as a Percentage of Enrollment in Public Schools of Sample Rural and Rural-Urban Counties and of Metropolitan Counties in Thirteen Southern States by Race, 1939-40, 1949-50, and 1951-52.................. 43

16. Changes in Enrollment in Sample Rural and Rural-Urban Counties, and in Metropolitan Counties of Thirteen Southern States by Race, 1939-40 to 1951-52 43

17. Median School Years Completed for Whites in United States, North and West, and South by Sex... 45

18. Median School Years Completed for Non-Whites for United States, North and West, and South by Sex.. 47

19. Number of Pupils in Average Daily Attendance per Classroom Teacher in Public Elementary and Secondary Schools of Twelve Southern States by Race, 1939-40 and 1951-52.. 49

20. Number of Pupils in Average Daily Attendance per Classroom Teacher in Public Elementary and Secondary Schools in Sample Rural and Rural-Urban Counties, and in Metropolitan Counties of Eight Southern States by Race, 1939-40 and 1951-52.. 49

21. Percentage of White and Negro Teachers with Specified Years of Training for Ten Southern States, 1939-40, 1949-50, and 1951-52.................. 51

22. Average Length in Days of the School Term in Public Schools in Twelve Southern States by Race, 1939-40, 1949-50, and 1951-52................ 53

23. Average Length in Days of the School Term in Public Schools in Sample Rural and Rural-Urban Counties, and in Metropolitan Counties in Twelve Southern States by Race, 1939-40, 1949-50, and 1951-52................. 53

24. Library Books per Pupil in ADA, in Southern States, 1939-40 to 1951-52.. 55

25. Library Expenditures per Pupil in Southern States, 1939-40 to 1951-52.. 55

26. Expenditures per Pupil Enrolled in Vocational Education in Public High Schools of Southern States by Race, 1939-40 and 1951-52, and Negro Expenditures as Percentage of White for 1951-52......................... 57

27. Pupils Enrolled in Vocational Programs per Thousand Pupils in High Schools of Southern States by Race, 1939-40 and 1951-52, and the Negro Enrollment as a Percentage of White, 1951-52......................... 57

28. Annual Salaries of Teachers in Rural and Rural-Urban Counties, and in Metropolitan Counties in the South by Race, 1939-40 and 1951-52......... 59

29. Annual Salaries of Teachers in South and Southern States by Race, 1939-40 and 1951-52.. 59

30. Public School Expenditures for South and Southern States, 1951-52...... 61

31. Expenditure per Pupil for Current Expenses Less Transportation for Six Southern States by Race, 1931-32 through 1951-52...................... 63

32. Total Current Expenditures for South and Southern States by Race, 1939-40 and 1951-52 65

33. Current Expenditures per Pupil in Average Daily Attendance for South and Southern States by Race, 1939-40 and 1951-52..................... 67

34. Current Expenditures per Pupil in Metropolitan Districts and Sample Rural Districts, and Rural as Percentage of Metropolitan, 1939-40 and 1951-52 69

35. Current Expenditures per Pupil in Metropolitan Districts and Sample Rural Districts by Race, 1951-52.. 69

36. Instruction as a Percentage of Current Expense in Public Schools of Six Southern States by Race, 1939-40 and 1951-52........................ 71

37. Median Ratios of Instruction Expenditures per White Pupil to Instruction Expenditures per Negro Pupil in Average Daily Attendance in Sample Rural and Rural-Urban, and in Metropolitan Counties with High and Low Percentages of Negro Population in Nine Southern States, 1939-40, 1949-50, and 1951-52 71

38. Expenditure per Pupil in Average Daily Attendance for Instruction in High and Low Income Sample Rural-Urban and Rural Counties and Metropolitan Counties by Race, 1939-40, 1949-50, and 1951-52............... 73

39. Expenditure per Pupil in Average Daily Attendance for Capital Outlay in the Public Schools of South and Southern States, 1939-40, 1949-50, and 1951-52, and Percentage Increase, 1939-40 to 1951-52.................... 75

40. Current Expenditures per Pupil in Average Daily Attendance in South and United States, Actual and Deflated, 1939-40 and 1949-50........... 77

41. 1960 School-Age Population, Ages 5-6, 7-13, 14-15, 16-17, and Total for South and Southern States by Race................................. 81

42. Basic and Adjusted Enrollment Ratios for South and Southern States to Be Applied in Enrollment Projection............................ 83

43. Projected 1960 Enrollment for South and Southern States According to the Projected Ratios 85

44. Ratio (Percentage) of Average Daily Attendance to Enrollment for Selected Years, 1909-1950, United States............................. 87

45. Average Daily Attendance for 1951-52 and the Projected Average Daily Attendance for 1959-60 for South and Southern States................. 89

46. Across-the-Board Equalization for South and Southern States, 1951-52... 91

47. Estimated Capital Deficits for South and Southern States in 1951-52.... 93

48. Annual Increments in Average Daily Attendance, Current and Transportation Expenditures for South and Southern States..................... 95

49. Total Costs for School Plant and Equipment for the South and Southern States, 1952-1960, and Annual Outlay over Eight Year Period.......... 97

50. Total Annual Costs of Equalized Current Expenditures, Transportation, and Equalized Schools and Equipment to Meet the Growth in Average Daily Attendance and Enrollment for South and Southern States........ 97

51. Per Capita Annual Income Payments in South and Non-South in Current Dollars and as a Percentage of 1929 and South as a Percentage of Non-South, 1929-1952 99

52. Income Payments to Individuals by Components as Percentage of Total Income and Percentage Change for United States and Southern States, 1929 and 1952 101

53. Total Income Payment Projections for South and Southern States under the Conservative Assumption, 1953-1960 103

54. Per Capita Income for Southern States Projected by High Income Assumption for 1953-1960.. 105

55. 1952 Total Income Payments and Projected High Total Income Payments for South and Southern States, 1953-1960............................ 105

56. Projected Total "High" Income Payments for South and Southern States Derived from the Per Capita Income for 1960 and Compared with Projected "Low" Income Payments 107

57. Total 1951-52 Current and Transportation Expenditures, the Costs of Equalization as of 1951-52 Across the Board, and the Annual Costs for Increments in Average Daily Attendance and Transportation for South and Southern States 109

58. Projection of Current and Transportation Expenditures for South and Southern States, 1952-1960 111

59. Amortization of Capital Deficit of $1,928 Millions Over a Twenty-Five Year Term at 3 Per Cent 113

60. Capital Deficits and Annual Amortization Payments for South and Southern States, 1951-52 115

61. Annual Capital Outlay to Meet School Enrollment Growth in South and Southern States, 1952-1960 117

62. Estimation of Fiscal Requirements to Meet Equalization Across the Board, Capital Deficits Funded, and the Growth in Capital and Current Needs in the South, 1951-1960 119

63. Projection of Total Outlays, Current, Transportation, and Capital, on the Assumption of Equalization Across the Board for South and Southern States, 1952-1960 121

64. Low and High Available Income and Total School Expenditures, 1952-53 through 1959-60 123

Public Education in the South Today and Tomorrow

Chapter 1

Introduction

The U. S. Supreme Court decision of May 17, 1954, holding segregation in the public schools unconstitutional, came in the midst of a period of revolutionary change in the South's educational system. The rapid economic growth of the region since the depression of the 1930's has brought not only the bi-racial aspects, but the whole of the South's public school system into a new focus. The unprecedented increase in resources for public schools has been more than matched by rising educational standards, expanding school population, and most important, by growing public demand for equal educational opportunity for all children, regardless of race or place of residence.

The Court's decision, redefining "equality" for Negro children as inclusion in a single, non-segregated system, has profound social significance for the South. But in terms of the improvement and expansion of school facilities and instruction, it is merely a special case within the overall pattern of change. The Southern states are launched on a vast program of educational equalization aimed at wiping out the old differentials between urban and rural, high-income and low-income areas, as well as between the races. And they are undertaking this huge task at a time when mounting school enrollments are straining existing facilities to the bursting point. Whatever economies or expenses, whatever pressure or relief, school integration may bring to Southern communities in the months and years to come, they will be overshadowed and in great part determined by the larger trends in Southern schooling.

The Investigation

Apart from the question of integration, the South is confronted by four major tasks in the field of public education:

1. equalization of current expenditures by race and by region
2. provision of modern housing for the existing group of pupils, also equalized by race and by region
3. improvement in instruction and enrichment programs to facilitate the transition from a predominantly agricultural to a predominantly industrial society
4. more classrooms and teachers to meet the huge advances in

enrollment and average daily attendance, which may be expected to reach a peak at the beginning of the next decade.

This last need arises from two developments in the region: the mounting increase in the school-age population and the large-scale shift of population from rural to urban areas and their peripheries, best termed "rurbanization."

In a democratic society educational goals are never static. The South today is experiencing the impact of broad social forces over which there appears to be little direct control. These forces have both complicated the educational problems of the South and given them an urgency which makes action imperative. Yet, the goals of action are uncertain, since no one can prescribe with certainty the best education for a region in which the basic cultural patterns are in flux. Recognizing these limitations, the participants in this largely statistical study of the educational problems of the South have aimed at the development of background material for the use of Southern educational leaders who must ultimately chart the course.

No attempt has been made to set forth *precisely* what ought to be done in each state. To do so would be sheer presumption, for the many educational programs involved must be geared to the needs and the capacity to pay of each particular state. But certain less specific diagnosis has been attempted. First, the total population growth has been analyzed to note the fundamental changes in its general composition—in particular, age, race, and residence. Second, the effects of these changes upon enrollment and average daily attendance have been projected to the end of the decade. Third, the school systems now in operation have been studied with a view to determining what and where are the deficiencies in the South's educational program. Fourth, the costs of providing equalized instruction and facilities for both races, for rural and urban children, and of wiping out existing deficits have been estimated by region and by state. Fifth, the fiscal requirements to meet the growing enrollment and average daily attendance are projected. Finally, the South's capacity to pay now and in the future is assessed; and time-tables have been developed to show for each state the expected date of "a balanced educational budget"—the date when educational expenses and total income payments allocated to education will come into balance.

These investigations have been prepared for the region as a whole and for each of the thirteen states here defined as comprising the South: Alabama, Arkansas, Florida, Georgia, Kentucky, Louisiana, Mississippi, North Carolina, Oklahoma, South Carolina, Tennessee, Texas, and Virginia. Also included are rural, rural-urban, and metropolitan school data drawn from school districts selected as representative of their respective areas. All metropolitan areas given by the United States Census are included, except for Texas, in which several sample metropolitan areas were selected. (See Appendix 1.)

Frequently, statistical comparisons are made with the accomplishments of the nation and the non-South. These comparisons do not necessarily serve as guides to action, but they do provide one measure of the status of public education in the South. It does not follow, however, that the educational problems of the South are the same as those elsewhere in the nation or that the goals are identical.

The effectiveness of public education can never be measured wholly in quantitative terms. The statement of educational goals in terms of dollars spent per pupil enrolled or in average daily attendance is an operational method that cannot pretend to define adequately either the quality or the intensity of education.

Regional differences in fund requirements are the rule and not the exception. Funds can surely be ineffectively applied, and they so often are that one school district with a relatively low per-pupil expenditure may actually be providing education superior to that provided by a school district spending many more dollars per pupil. A dollar spent per child in Cook County, Illinois, or in Manhattan Borough could not conceivably yield the same level of education as a dollar spent per pupil in Fulton County, Georgia, or in Waco, Texas.

Thus the dollar measure must always be viewed, at best, as a crude index to the quality of an educational program.

The Findings

To be sure, some states, some counties, and some cities in the South have met, or have more than met, the challenge posed by comparison with other regions. But the South as a whole suffers from a sizable deficiency in public education. In most of the Southern states, neither the white nor the Negro segment of the population has received an education on a par with that to be had elsewhere in the nation. Cumulative inequalities since the decade of the 1870's have limited the Negro's educational opportunities even more than the white's. In recent times, concerted action to narrow the gap between the races has yielded substantial results, but the gap is still far from closed in most states. In some, where the racial differential is rapidly disappearing, efforts are now being directed toward raising and enriching the general level of education.

All of these efforts are made doubly difficult by the unprecedented rate of growth in enrollment and average daily attendance resulting from the spectacular rise in the school-age population. As late as 1950, the total school-age population was no greater than it was in 1930, for during the late 1930's and the 1940's a major out-migration occurred. But since the end of World War II, mounting birth rates have pushed the school-age population upward toward an anticipated peak in 1960 for the elementary school group, and in about 1962 for the secondary school group. This development is further complicated by the great migration from rural to urban areas that began during the 1940's. This "rurbanization" is the by-product of the growing industrialization and the shift to mechanized farming in the South.

Nearly twelve and a half million Southerners live outside their home states, and of this large number nearly seven and a half million now make their homes in the non-South. Yet this great loss of population has been partly counterbalanced by another development: over three million non-Southerners have moved into the region, and as migration continues the South is acquiring more and more people from the non-South. Compound these interregional movements with the shifts to the cities and city peripheries, and a total migration of some fifteen and a half million people has occurred in recent decades.

The Negro has participated more than the white in this great flow of people. During the 1940's about two-thirds of the increase in the net migratory loss of the South was accounted for by the movement of Negroes to Northern industrial centers.

The full impact of these population changes upon education is only beginning to be felt.

While much has been done in recent years to achieve greater equalization and improvement of public education and to meet the growth of enrollment and average daily attendance, much more remains to be done. The increase in educational costs as a result of the vast population and industrial developments must of necessity be staggering.

In order to project these costs, conditions existing in the fiscal year 1951-52 and preceding years have been reviewed. The year 1951-52 was selected as the base year for all the investigations into the actual operations of the schools and all the projections. At the time the study was initiated, 1951-52 was then the latest year for which all data needed were available. This choice of base year permits a comparison of forecasts with actual developments in the immediately succeeding years, data for which are currently becoming available.

In 1951-52, current expenditures, excluding transportation outlays, per pupil in average daily attendance averaged for the white children in the South $165.71 and for the Negro $115.56. Thus at the outset a gap in current expenditures of $50 per Negro pupil remained to be closed.

This gap reflects differences in various expenditures. In 1951-52, the average salary paid white teachers in the South had reached $1,460, while for Negro teachers it was $1,273—a difference of $187 per teacher. Qualitative variations are also apparent. As late as 1951-52, some 9 per cent of Negro teachers in the region had less than two years of special training, whereas only 3.3 per cent of the white teachers fall into this class. Some 73 per cent of the Negro teachers had four or more years of training, as compared with about 78 per cent of the white teachers.

In public school libraries, there were fewer books per Negro pupil than per white. For seven states reporting, the ratio was 4.3 books per white pupil and only 2.0 books per Negro pupil.

Of the total expenditures in 1951-52, instructional outlays accounted for a much higher proportion of the expenditure per Negro pupil than of that per white pupil. This reflects the tendency in the South to put more into the enrichment programs for white than for Negro school children.

Comparable to the differentials between white and Negro pupils are those related to place of residence. There are sizable dollar gaps between expenditures per pupil in rural, rural-urban, and metropolitan areas. Based on sample studies, instructional expenditure per metropolitan child exceeded the expenditure per rural-urban child by $36.40 and exceeded the expenditure per rural child by $44.05.

In 1951-52, the average expenditure per white pupil in the South was $166. This regional average—or the actual state expenditure per white pupil where it is higher—is a realistic target figure in estimating the cost of equalization. On this basis, to equalize current expenditures in the South for all children, white and Negro, as of 1951-52 would cost a total of $210 million. One state, Oklahoma, has already achieved equalization at approximately $196 per pupil. Two states—Texas and Florida—are approaching the goal of $166 for Negroes and whites.

Until quite recently, capital expenditures on buildings and equipment per pupil have likewise tended to run significantly more for the white than for the Negro children. Relative to the enrollment by race, out of an estimated total capital deficiency for the region of nearly two billion dollars in 1951-52, approximately 40 per cent, or about $800 million, must be spent to improve, replace, and supplement schools serving Negro pupils. This deficit applies only to the existing school-age population and takes no account of anticipated increases.

The rises in rurban population and the school-age population set the basic patterns of enrollment. The enrollment trend is in three directions: upward in all grades; toward the city schools; and in Southern cities and their metropolitan areas, particularly toward the secondary schools. A net public school enrollment of nearly 8,300,000 was reached in the South in 1950, the last census year. By 1960 the net enrollment is expected to reach 10,748,000. By age groups, the enrollments in 1960 will probably be: for 5-6 years, 825,000; for 7-13 years, 7,076,000; for 14-15, 1,542,000; and for 16-17, 1,305,000.

In 1950 average daily attendance in the South was approximately 7,240,000. But this figure is expected to reach nearly 9,800,000 by 1960, an estimated increase of 35.3 per cent in average daily attendance. This estimate is fairly consistent with the expected rise of 29.5 per cent in enrollment, when adjusted for the effects of anticipated improvements in instruction and facilities.

To meet the rise in current expenditures imposed by the growth of average daily attendance, under the present system, the South as a whole would have to provide for an annual increase of around $46,847,000 until 1960. To meet the same rise in transportation expenses would require an annual increase estimated at $3,121,000. The total of the two increments would reach as much as $14,658,000 for Texas and as little as $1,643,000 for Mississippi, a difference which reflects the variations in school-age population in those states.

In addition, whatever system is employed, the South must provide more buildings and equipment to accommodate the growing number of pupils. The annual outlay for this purpose should run as high as $161,889,000 for the region as a whole. The greatest outlay will be required of Texas, some $41,572,000. By 1960, the South will have paid out a total of more than $1,295,000,000 for additional plants and equipment.

Incorporated in the estimates of both current and capital expenditures is an allowance for improvement of instruction and facilities.

Can the South Afford This Program?

The pertinent question, of course, is whether the Southern people can afford this extensive program to improve their schools while providing for an unprecedented growth in enrollment and average daily attendance. The answer is an optimistic, but qualified, yes. *If* equalization is defined in terms of the region's average current expediture per white pupil in average daily attendance ($166) or the present state expenditure per white pupil when higher than $166; *if* essentially the same modernized space and equipment is to be provided for each student; and *if* the present trend in regional income continues—then the South can provide a tolerably good program.

Obviously, the criteria used in this study are arbitrary, as would be any others selected. For example, the amount of space allowed per pupil—45 square feet in elementary and 60 square feet in secondary schools—represents a judgment on the space necessary for adequate plant facilities. In like fashion, as discussed above, the region's average current expenditure per white pupil in average daily attendance is an arbitrary target figure. What the South has done for its white school children seemed to be a realistic goal for those states which have not yet achieved it for all children.

The South experienced from 1938 to 1952 a phenomenal growth in real per capita income; that is, income stated in a constant dollar so that the effect of changes in the general price level are removed from the current dollar figures. This growth has averaged over 5 per cent annually for the region. The consequence is a higher capacity to meet public school needs.

Two income estimates for the period 1952-1960 were developed, one conservative and one optimistic. The first rests upon the assumption that the region's average income will not continue to advance at 5 per cent per annum but will drop to the long-run growth average of the United States as a whole; 3.2 per cent per annum is the resulting figure. The optimistic assumption, based on the trend established for the period 1938-1952, assumes that the growth will continue to average 5 per cent per annum. In either case, of course, some states will exceed and some will fall below the average.

By the conservative assumption, total income payments in the South in 1960 will reach $67,200,000,000. By the optimistic assumption, the expected total income in 1960 is $85,000,000,000.

The South's capacity to pay for the school program defined above is computed by multiplying each series of total income payment projections by 3.3 per cent. (This percentage represents the past relative outlay out of income by the Southern states for educational expenditures, current, transportation, and debt amortization and interest.) Thus a range of capacity to pay is derived, with 3.3 per cent times the conservative income series and 3.3 per cent times the optimistic series stating the lower and upper limits. These ranges have been computed for the South as a region and for each state in the region.

Five of the states will be able to defray from the beginning the expected total costs for the period under either income condition. These are Florida, Kentucky, Oklahoma, Texas, and Virginia. By 1960 every state but one will be able, under the optimistic assumption of income, to meet all of its projected expenditures. The single exception, Mississippi, should reach its break-even point, where income allocated to education meets the total educational costs, by 1963.

Other states may further improve and enrich their programs with the "surplus" income allocated to education and not applied under the assumptions set forth here. More than half of the states could thus enter upon fairly extensive improvement plans.

On the whole, the prospects for Southern education are, according to these findings, far brighter than many have supposed. The economic advance of the South has made much more programming possible than had hitherto been contemplated. Moreover, this process tends to be self-generating. As the region advances economically, education is improved; as education is improved, the productivity of the South's people is increased; and this, in turn, brings further economic advance. To be sure, the process of economic development is sometimes fickle; but the chances are good that the present rate of growth of 5 per cent will be continued into the 1960's with but one or two minor fluctuations from the trend so set.

Here and in the pages that follow, racial data have been presented largely in terms of the existing dual school systems. In the case of past developments, this was an obvious necessity, since the two races have been served by separate school facilities in the thirteen states discussed. Estimates of future needs and developments are cast in the same form as a matter of convenience. In no other way could equalization of educational opportunities by race be meaningfully treated.

The editors have made no assumptions about the timing or extent of integration in the aftermath of the Supreme Court's public school rulings; such considerations fall outside the scope of this survey. The editors have assumed, however, that the goal of Southern school systems is the elimination of inequalities in facilities and instruction for all children. Accordingly, the measurement of deficits and projected expenditures in terms of the existing dual systems is a valid procedure. For the cost of eliminating these differentials for the region as a whole and for the individual states will be approximately the same, whether accomplished within a system of segregation, integration, or a combination of the two.

True, integration may effect some economies in specific local situations—particularly where the percentage of Negroes is small. But such economies, while they may bulk large in the given community, are not statistically significant in regional or even in state-wide terms. In these broad settings, possible savings through integration are dwarfed by the overall demands of public education in a period of great population and economic changes.

Public discussion of the Supreme Court's decision in the South has been mainly centered on its social and political implications. Increasingly, however, it must be viewed in the context of education as the biggest and most expensive public function of the Southern states. Educators, public officials, and private citizens seeking detailed solutions to the problems of bi-racial education will proceed the more soundly if they see before them the full dimensions of the public-school effort that lies ahead. To the extent that this volume helps them in that undertaking, it will have achieved its purpose.

Part One

Public Education in the South Today

Chapter 2

The People of the South

THE POPULATION OF THE SOUTH

The thirteen states of the South occupy 29 per cent of the continental United States (862,867 of 3,022,387 square miles). Their combined population in 1950 was 41,728,272, or 27.7 per cent of the nation's total population. Southerners were concentrated 43.7 to the square mile in contrast to a concentration of 50.7 persons per square mile for the continental United States. The range in gross area was from South Carolina's 31,055 square miles to Texas' 267,339. In population, the range was from Arkansas, with 1,909,511, to Texas, with 7,711,194.

The Southern people, more than those of other regions, have been predominately native-born Americans, and, more than most, born in their own region. Southern whites came primarily from British stocks, and Negroes from the West Coast of Africa. Historically the Southern people, black and white, have been rural, and population increases have been related to this rural characteristic and the accompanying patterns of fertility.

In the colonial period the people of the South constituted half of the American population, but the rising tide of western migration shifted the center of population. In the first census decade, Southern population increased more rapidly than the nation's population, but in the sixteen subsequent decennial periods the South has exceeded the national rate only twice.

Recent changes in the population of the region are associated with the urban trend, interregional migration (particularly Negro migration), and declining fertility.

TABLE 1

Population of United States, Non-South, South, and Southern States by Decades, 1900-1950

[*Figures given to nearest 1,000 population*]

	1900	1910	1920	1930	1940	1950
United States	75,643	91,972	105,711	122,775	131,669	150,697
Non-South	53,730	64,753	76,159	89,003	94,656	109,969
South	21,913	26,340	29,552	33,772	37,013	41,728
Alabama	1,829	2,138	2,348	2,646	2,833	3,062
Arkansas	1,312	1,574	1,752	1,854	1,949	1,910
Florida	529	753	968	1,468	1,897	2,771
Georgia	2,216	2,609	2,896	2,909	3,124	3,445
Kentucky	2,147	2,290	2,417	2,615	2,846	2,945
Louisiana	1,382	1,656	1,799	2,102	2,364	2,684
Mississippi	1,551	1,797	1,791	2,010	2,184	2,179
N. Carolina	1,894	2,206	2,559	3,170	3,572	4,062
Oklahoma	790	1,657	2,028	2,396	2,336	2,233
S. Carolina	1,340	1,515	1,684	1,739	1,900	2,117
Tennessee	2,021	2,185	2,338	2,617	2,916	3,292
Texas	3,049	3,897	4,663	5,825	6,415	7,711
Virginia	1,854	2,062	2,309	2,422	2,678	3,319

SOURCE: U.S. Census of Population, 1950.

THE GROWTH OF THE SOUTHERN PEOPLE

The decennial rates of increase in the population of the Southern states as seen in Table 2 reflect the nearly unique role of the South in the growth of the American people. This region has maintained higher levels of fertility than the other major regions and has exported to other regions a major portion of its excess population. Thus the South has come to be known as the "seedbed" of the nation.

For a century and a half the center of balance of the American people has moved westward. With the growing importance of these western regions, the Northeast and the South have become steadily less important in the numerical distribution of population. This has come about, however, through a more involved process than a simple westward movement. The Northeast has sent many of its inhabitants westward and has had a continuous replenishment during the past census periods from the South. The North Central region has also sent many persons westward and for more than a century has had a constant flow of migrants from the South. Meanwhile, Southern migrants have moved westward also; so the migration from the region has flowed in three directions.

As a result of this multiple migration pattern, the region has grown more slowly than the nation throughout its history, except for the first census decade, and for 1890 to 1900 and 1930 to 1940, when both birth rates and migration were slowed by the forces of depression. The extent of the difference in rates of growth during the present century appears in Table 2. In the decade 1940 to 1950 only three of the states in the region had greater increases than the nation —Florida, Texas, and Virginia. Only Texas and Florida have had consistently larger percentages of growth than the nation during the half century, and only these two states have exceeded their net rates of natural increase through the fifty years.

It should be pointed out that the relatively small increase in total population does not apply to the school-age population, for most of the emigrants from the region have been persons who have completed most or all of their formal education before migrating. Thus the region's public schools have had to serve a larger proportion of children than the total size of the population would indicate.

TABLE 2

Percentage Changes in Total Population for United States, Non-South, South, and Southern States by Decades, 1900-1950

	Per Cent Change				
	1900-1910	1910-1920	1920-1930	1930-1940	1940-1950
United States.........	21.0	14.9	16.1	7.2	14.5
Non-South.............	21.4	16.0	16.9	6.4	15.1
South.................	20.2	12.2	14.3	9.6	12.7
Alabama............	16.9	9.8	12.7	7.0	8.1
Arkansas...........	20.0	11.3	5.8	5.1	−2.0
Florida.............	42.4	28.7	51.6	29.2	46.1
Georgia.............	17.7	11.0	.4	7.4	10.3
Kentucky...........	6.6	5.5	8.2	8.8	3.5
Louisiana...........	19.9	8.6	16.9	12.5	13.5
Mississippi..........	15.8	−.4	12.2	8.7	−.2
N. Carolina.........	16.5	16.0	23.9	12.7	13.7
Oklahoma...........	109.7	22.4	18.1	−2.5	−4.4
S. Carolina..........	13.1	11.1	3.3	9.3	11.4
Tennessee...........	8.1	7.0	11.9	11.4	12.9
Texas...............	27.8	19.7	24.9	10.1	20.2
Virginia.............	11.2	12.0	4.9	10.6	23.9

Source: U.S. Census of Population, 1950.

THE PERCENTAGE OF NEGROES IN THE POPULATION

The American Negro has sometimes been called "America's tenth man." Table 3 shows that from 1900 to 1950 Negroes have steadily represented about 10 per cent of the people of the United States, but the Negro population by state and by region during the half century has undergone a widespread redistribution.

From the time of the discovery of the cotton gin to the end of the Civil War, most of the Negroes in the United States were found in the South, particularly in the cotton South where slave labor came to be regarded as an essential factor in the plantation economy. By 1900 some 85 per cent of the Negroes in the United States were still living in the Southern states and were still heavily concentrated in the fertile crescent where cotton flourished.

From 1900 to 1950 redistribution of Negroes in the United States was so great that the percentage of American Negroes living in the South was cut from 85 per cent to 62.5 per cent. Whereas in 1900 one out of three Southerners were Negroes, in 1950 only two out of nine Southern persons were Negroes. On the other hand, in 1900 about two persons out of a hundred in the non-South were Negroes, but by 1950 five out of every hundred persons were Negroes.

In 1900 Negroes exceeded 40 per cent of the population in six "deep South" states, but by 1950 Negroes exceeded 40 per cent only in one—Mississippi—and even there the proportion had declined from 58.5 to 45.4 per cent.

Thus the Negro as a percentage of United States population has changed little in 50 years, but his distribution among the states and regions has undergone profound changes. This reshuffling of the Negro population has had significant implications for the problems of education.

TABLE 3

Negro Population as a Percentage of the Total Population for United States, Non-South, South, and Southern States by Decades, 1900-1950

	1900	1910	1920	1930	1940	1950
United States	11.6	10.7	9.9	9.7	9.8	10.0
Non-South	2.3	2.3	2.6	4.3	3.8	5.1
South	34.8	31.7	28.6	23.8	25.0	22.5
Alabama	45.2	42.5	38.4	25.7	34.7	32.1
Arkansas	28.0	28.1	27.0	25.8	24.7	22.3
Florida	43.7	41.0	34.0	29.4	27.1	21.7
Georgia	46.7	45.1	41.7	36.8	34.7	30.9
Kentucky	13.3	11.4	9.8	8.6	7.5	6.9
Louisiana	47.1	43.1	38.9	36.9	35.9	32.9
Mississippi	58.5	56.2	52.2	50.2	49.2	45.4
N. Carolina	33.0	31.6	29.8	29.0	27.5	25.8
Oklahoma	7.0*	8.3	7.4	7.2	7.2	6.5
S. Carolina	58.4	55.2	51.4	45.6	42.8	38.8
Tennessee	23.8	21.7	19.3	18.3	17.4	16.1
Texas	20.4	17.7	15.9	14.7	14.4	12.7
Virginia	35.6	32.6	29.9	26.8	24.7	22.1

SOURCE: *Negroes in the United States*, 1900 to 1932; U.S. Censuses of Population, 1940 and 1950.
*Includes population of Indian Territory.

THE COMPARISON OF THE RATES OF INCREASE OF WHITE AND NEGRO POPULATION

The fact that the nation's population has increased at a faster rate than that of the South in all but three census decades since 1790 conceals a racial differential. For, as Table 4 reveals, Southern whites have consistently increased at a faster rate than whites in the non-South. The total Southern increase falls below the non-South figure, however, because of the significantly lower Negro rate of increase in the South.

This is attributable, of course, to the heavy movement of Southern Negroes to urban centers outside the region. The effects of this movement are evident in the steep rate of Negro increase in the non-South—a total of 332 per cent between 1900 and 1950.

The Southern trend is long established, for not since slavery days have Negroes increased more rapidly than whites; only from 1810 to 1830 did this occur. But the Negro's declining rate of increase has been particularly significant in the South since 1900. During the fifty-year period in only two decades, 1900-1910, 1930-1940, the Negro rate of increase approached half the white rate of increase, and by the decade 1940-1950 the Negro rate of increase in the thirteen states was less than one-tenth of the white. For the entire half century the Negro rate of increase—approximately 25 per cent—was only one-fifth the white rate of 125 per cent.

Among the Southern states only North Carolina had a Negro rate of increase comparable to its white increase. Florida had the most rapid increase of all the Southern states; yet the white increase exceeded the Negro by three times.

Among Southern people, there is a popular belief that Negroes constitute half the population and that they are increasing more rapidly than white. As Table 3 shows, Negroes make up less than one-fourth the South's total population, and it is only in the non-Southern states receiving migration from the South that the Negro rate of increase exceeds the white.

TABLE 4

Percentage Change of Population for United States, Non-South, South, and Southern States by Decades by Race, 1900-1950

	1910		1920		1930		1940		1950		Percentage Change 1900-1950	
	White	Negro	White	Negro	White	Negro	White	Negro	White	Negro	White	Negro
United States..	22.3	11.2	16.0	6.5	16.3	13.6	7.2	8.2	14.1	16.9	102.0	70.3
Non-South....	21.5	14.8	15.7	34.8	15.8	52.6	6.0	16.8	13.4	56.6	95.7	331.7
South........	25.2	10.6	17.4	1.4	18.1	4.3	11.3	5.2	16.5	1.5	125.1	24.9
Alabama....	22.7	9.8	17.8	−0.9	17.5	4.9	8.7	4.1	12.5	−0.4	107.7	18.7
Arkansas....	19.7	20.7	13.2	6.6	7.5	1.3	6.6	0.9	1.1	−11.6	56.8	16.6
Florida.....	49.2	33.8	43.8	6.7	62.2	31.1	33.5	19.1	56.7	17.3	528.5	161.8
Georgia.....	21.2	13.7	18.0	2.5	8.8	−11.2	11.0	1.3	16.8	−2.0	101.5	2.8
Kentucky...	8.9	−8.1	7.5	−9.8	9.5	−4.2	10.2	−5.3	4.2	−5.7	47.2	−28.8
Louisiana...	29.0	9.7	16.5	−1.9	20.6	10.9	14.3	9.4	18.8	3.9	146.3	36.0
Mississippi..	22.6	11.2	8.6	−7.4	16.9	8.0	10.8	6.4	7.4	−8.2	84.5	8.8
N. Carolina.	18.7	11.7	18.9	9.4	25.3	20.3	14.9	6.8	16.2	10.7	136.1	71.2
Oklahoma...	115.5	145.3	26.1	8.6	17.0	15.3	−1.2	−2.0	−3.4	−13.8	203.3	161.3
S. Carolina..	21.8	6.8	20.5	3.5	15.3	−8.2	14.9	2.6	19.3	1.0	131.9	5.3
Tennessee...	11.1	−1.5	10.2	−4.5	13.4	5.7	12.5	6.5	14.7	4.3	79.2	10.6
Texas......	32.1	11.2	22.3	7.5	26.8	15.3	10.5	8.1	22.6	5.7	177.2	57.5
Virginia.....	16.5	1.6	16.4	2.8	9.4	−5.8	13.8	1.7	28.1	11.0	116.4	11.5

Source: U.S. Census of Population, 1950.

FROM FARM TO CITY

The increase of the urban population and the accompanying decline of the rural population of the South since 1900 reflect the accelerating growth of Southern cities and their suburbs. From 1900 to 1950 the rate of increase of the urban population of the South was more than double the national rate. Over the half century the United States urban population increased 190 per cent, as against 436 per cent for the South. During this same period the rural population of the United States increased 25 per cent, while the Southern increase was 28 per cent. Thus the population growth in the South has been like that of the nation, but because the culture and the history of the region have been primarily associated with the rural way of life, the Southern gains in urbanization are more significant.

Table 5 reveals that the proportion of Southerners living in urban places has increased three times since 1900. Put another way, only fifteen Southerners out of the hundred were living in urban places of residence in 1900, but by 1950 urban dwellers and rural dwellers were almost equally divided, whether by the old census definition of urban or by the new.

The sociological significance of the urban trend in the South is rendered more dramatic when it is noted that in addition to movement toward the city, there is interchange of population between farms and non-farm areas. The migration from farms to non-farm residences was estimated at nearly ten million from 1940 to 1949 and the migration from non-farm to farm residences at approximately five million. The total number of moves was approximately fifteen million. Such movement between farm and non-farm places of residence, added to the movement toward the city, has resulted in a far-reaching diffusion of urban cultural patterns. This has been particularly apparent in the changing definition of equality of educational opportunities—whether between rural and urban or Negro and white.

TABLE 5

Percentage of Total Population Urban or Rural for United States, South, and Southern States by Decades, 1900-1950

	1900		1910		1920		1930		1940		1950*			
											A		B	
	Urban	Rural	Urban	Rural	Urban	Rural	Urban	Rural	Urban	Rural	Urban	Rural	Urban	Rural
United States...	39.7	60.3	45.7	54.3	51.2	48.8	54.2	43.8	56.5	43.5	59.0	41.0	64.0	36.0
South..........	15.2	84.8	20.2	79.8	25.4	74.6	32.1	67.9	35.1	65.2	42.9	57.1	47.1	52.9
Alabama.....	11.0	89.0	17.3	82.7	21.7	78.3	28.1	71.9	30.2	69.8	40.1	59.9	43.8	56.2
Arkansas.....	8.5	91.5	12.9	87.1	16.6	83.4	20.6	79.4	22.2	77.2	32.3	67.7	33.0	67.0
Florida......	20.3	79.7	29.1	69.9	36.5	63.5	51.7	48.3	55.1	44.9	56.5	43.5	65.5	34.5
Georgia......	15.6	84.4	20.6	79.4	25.1	74.9	30.8	69.2	34.4	65.6	40.1	59.9	45.3	54.7
Kentucky....	21.8	78.2	24.3	75.7	26.2	73.8	30.6	69.4	29.8	70.2	33.5	66.5	36.8	63.2
Louisiana....	26.5	74.5	30.0	70.0	34.9	65.1	39.7	60.3	41.5	58.5	50.8	49.2	54.8	45.2
Mississippi...	7.7	92.3	11.5	88.5	13.4	86.6	16.9	83.1	19.8	80.2	27.6	72.4	27.9	72.1
N. Carolina..	9.9	91.1	14.4	85.6	19.2	80.8	25.5	74.5	27.3	72.7	30.5	69.5	33.7	66.3
Oklahoma....	7.4	92.6	19.2	80.8	26.5	73.5	34.3	65.7	37.6	62.4	49.6	50.4	51.0	49.0
S. Carolina...	12.8	87.2	14.8	85.2	17.5	82.5	21.3	78.7	24.5	75.5	28.8	71.2	36.7	63.3
Tennessee....	13.5	86.5	16.2	83.8	26.1	73.9	34.3	65.7	35.2	64.8	38.4	61.6	44.1	55.9
Texas........	17.1	82.9	24.1	75.9	32.4	67.6	41.0	59.0	45.4	54.6	59.8	40.2	62.7	37.3
Virginia......	18.3	81.7	23.1	76.9	29.2	70.8	32.4	67.6	35.3	64.7	40.3	59.7	47.0	53.0

SOURCE: U.S. Census of Population, 1950.
*Column A, 1950, "Urban," according to the 1930 and 1940 definition: Only persons living within the corporate limits of incorporated places of 2,500 or more persons and in areas indicated as urban by special designation. All others, rural. Column B, 1950, "Urban," according to the 1950 definition: Persons living within the places of urban size, 2,500 or over, without regard to incorporation and persons in densely settled areas adjacent to urban places or cities. All others, rural.

WHITE AND NEGRO RATES OF URBANIZATION

The long-time urban trend in the nation and in the South was slowed somewhat during the depression decade of 1930-1940, but from 1940 to 1950 under the impact of war, mechanization of farming, and the expanding economy, the movement toward the city was greatly accelerated. As Table 6 shows, the white urban increase in the South was 43.4 per cent, as compared with 26.2 per cent for Negroes.

It was not many years ago that the typical Negro living in the South was a rural-farm resident, but by 1950 nearly half of the Negro population of the South was living in cities or other urban places. The percentage of urban increase among Negroes from 1940 to 1950 is reported at approximately 26 per cent and the white at approximately 43 per cent. Hidden in these statistics are two important trends: the Southern Negro was moving to cities outside the region, and more whites than Negroes were moving to Southern cities from outside the South. Thus, despite the fact that the white urban increase in the South greatly exceeded the Negro urban increase, the movement of Southern Negroes to cities—North and South—paralleled or exceeded that of Southern whites.

Negroes moving to standard metropolitan areas have concentrated in the central city sections. Although only 63 per cent of the white urban dwellers live in the central cities, 74 per cent of Negroes live in these areas. This reflects the tendency of white families to make their homes in the suburbs—a tendency not shared by Negroes for socio-economic reasons. When the Negro minority takes over the congested central city areas, numerous public facilities, such as schools, formerly used by whites, are changed over to Negro use. Because of residential segregation in many metropolitan places, a high degree of public school segregation will probably continue regardless of legal developments toward integration and Negroes will be using the second-hand facilities, while whites occupy the newer schools nearer the periphery of the cities.

[25]

TABLE 6

Percentage Change in Urban, Rural Non-Farm, and Rural Farm Population for United States, Non-South, South, and Southern States by Race, 1940-1950

	URBAN*		RURAL NON-FARM		RURAL FARM	
	White	Negro	White	Negro	White	Negro
United States	17.3	43.5	43.4	40.4	−22.5	−29.8
Non-South	12.9	60.7	41.7	59.6	−19.4	−30.9
South	43.4	26.2	47.8	34.5	−26.4	−29.7
Alabama	51.2	30.4	38.5	32.4	−25.4	−33.3
Arkansas	45.4	35.2	23.3	9.4	−25.7	−33.7
Florida	57.4	29.8	97.7	18.4	−20.0	−29.0
Georgia	32.0	22.6	70.3	35.7	−26.1	−34.9
Kentucky	17.6	6.3	36.4	−4.7	−21.9	−39.1
Louisiana	41.4	34.3	38.7	46.5	−29.0	−38.3
Mississippi	45.3	30.1	38.9	32.6	−19.5	−23.3
N. Carolina	31.3	17.6	57.6	39.5	−19.0	−11.7
Oklahoma	27.3	13.0	8.0	9.1	−39.5	−47.4
S. Carolina	37.2	19.4	51.6	62.8	−21.5	−24.6
Tennessee	25.4	17.0	69.0	19.5	−19.5	−23.4
Texas	62.1	36.8	31.7	45.9	−38.4	−47.0
Virginia	46.5	26.6	69.0	58.4	−23.4	−31.4

SOURCE: U.S. Census of Population, 1950.
*Old urban definition.

THE UNEVENNESS OF SOUTHERN POPULATION GROWTH

The growth of population in the South is far from uniform throughout the states and counties of the region. The overall increase of 12.7 per cent in the population of the Southern states from 1940 to 1950 would seem to point toward a generally expanding population base for the whole region. But in fact the South has for many years, and particularly during the last census period, been a mosaic of contrasting population trends, with increases and decreases scattered across the maps of the individual states. This unevenness of population change is seen in the fact that 714 Southern counties lost population from 1940 to 1950 and 619 gained population.

Of the counties losing population, more than a hundred lost 20 per cent or more and 380 lost 10 per cent or more of their 1940 population. The total of 714 counties showing decreases lost approximately 12 per cent of their population during the decade. On the other hand, the 619 counties showing gains increased their population by approximately 26 per cent. Over one-third of the counties gaining increased their population by more than 20 per cent.

Among the declining counties, more than half had no urban population in either 1940 or 1950, and the remainder had only small urban populations. There was no predominately urban county in the group.

By contrast only 112 of the 619 counties increasing had no urban population, and there was a strong association between the percentage of urban and the percentage of 1940-1950 growth. An overwhelming majority of the urban population of the South was located in the growing counties, and the rural percentages in these counties were far

TABLE 7

Population by Counties Increasing and Counties Decreasing and Percentage Change for South and Southern States, 1940-1950

[Population figures given to nearest 1,000 persons]

	Counties Showing Increase				Counties Showing Decrease			
	Number of Counties	Total Population		Percentage Change	Number of Counties	Total Population		Percentage Change
		1940	1950			1940	1950	
South	619	24,018	30,248	25.94	714	12,995	11,481	−11.65
Alabama	23	1,600	1,936	20.97	45	1,233	1,126	− 8.67
Arkansas	19	857	952	11.14	56	1,092	957	−12.39
Florida	49	1,738	2,622	51.40	18	165	149	− 9.86
Georgia	61	1,907	2,342	22.80	98	1,217	1,103	− 9.37
Kentucky	42	1,534	1,757	14.51	78	1,311	1,188	− 9.41
Louisiana	34	1,713	2,095	22.29	30	651	588	− 9.57
Mississippi	23	775	899	15.95	59	1,408	1,280	− 9.13
N. Carolina	78	3,257	3,763	15.56	22	315	299	− 5.19
Oklahoma	11	708	908	28.18	66	1,628	1,326	−18.58
S. Carolina	31	1,572	1,808	15.01	15	328	309	− 5.70
Tennessee	52	2,190	2,621	19.68	43	726	671	− 7.60
Texas	108	3,965	5,664	42.84	146	2,450	2,047	−16.42
Virginia	88	2,207	2,880	30.51	38	471	439	− 6.87

Source: Bureau of the Census, 1950 Census of Population, Advance Reports, Series PC-8.

lower than those of the losing counties. Furthermore the average population of the counties gaining was three times that of the counties losing. Thus most of the population growth between 1940 and 1950 took place in areas that were already urban at the beginning of the decade.

Urbanization dominated the growth pattern in the South more clearly than in the nation as a whole. The South with 43 per cent of the nation's counties had 39 per cent of all the counties showing increases from 1940 to 1950 and 47 per cent of all the counties showing decreases. However, the Southern counties which increased 20 per cent or more made up well over one-third of all the Southern counties showing increases, while the same category of the United States outside the South was well below one-third of the total. Of the 32 counties in the United States showing increases of 100 per cent or more, 19 were in the South. The concentration of Southern population growth is further indicated by the disproportionate number of Southern cities in the group of American cities with increases of 100 per cent or more.

In summary, without regard to rates of growth of the states as entities, the large counties of the South show rapid growth, comprehend most of the recent population increase of the region, and are assuming an ever greater importance in terms of their share of the total population of the region.

The implications for both local and state governments and for public services, such as education, are apparent. While making adjustments to meet falling population in more than half of their county units, the states of the region must simultaneously provide for increasing population in other counties.

TABLE 8

Distribution of Counties Showing Population Increases and Decreases by Percentage Changes for United States, Non-South, South and Southern States, 1940-1950

	DISTRIBUTION OF COUNTIES BY PERCENTAGE INCREASE					DISTRIBUTION OF COUNTIES BY PERCENTAGE DECREASE				
	0.0 to 4.9	5.0 to 9.9	10.0 to 19.9	20 Per Cent or more	Total	0.0 to 4.9	5.0 to 9.9	10.0 to 19.9	20 Per Cent or more	Total
United States...	394	307	364	520	1,585	414	396	520	188	1,518
Non-South.....	243	195	236	292	966	257	219	264	64	804
South.........	151	112	128	228	619	157	177	256	124	714
Alabama....	7	3	1	9	23	11	9	22	2	44
Arkansas....	8	3	5	3	19	8	12	20	16	56
Florida......	4	2	10	33	49	7	3	6	2	18
Georgia.....	16	12	12	21	61	22	31	39	6	98
Kentucky...	17	13	7	5	42	20	17	34	7	78
Louisiana....	5	9	11	9	34	7	9	11	3	30
Mississippi ..	9	5	5	4	23	13	18	24	4	59
N. Carolina..	19	23	21	15	78	10	9	3	—	22
Oklahoma...	1	2	1	7	11	3	8	22	33	66
S. Carolina..	7	9	8	7	31	5	8	2	—	15
Tennessee...	20	8	12	12	52	13	18	10	2	43
Texas.......	12	12	18	66	108	19	23	56	48	146
Virginia.....	26	11	14	37	88	19	12	7	1	39

SOURCE: Bureau of the Census, 1950 Census of Population, Advance Reports, Series PC-8.

THE MOVEMENT OF PEOPLE IN THE SOUTHERN STATES

The effects of interregional migration on the population of the South are shown in Table 9. A total of 12,444,310 persons who were born in the thirteen Southern states and living outside the state of their birth in 1950 represents 35.3 per cent of the nation's net interstate migrants, a disproportionately large share for the region. Of these twelve million, some 5,100,185 had moved from one Southern state to another; 7,344,125 had moved to a non-Southern state.

Meanwhile, 8,127,905 persons born in other states were living in the thirteen Southern states, 3,027,720 of them natives of states outside the South. Thus interregional movement to and from the South had affected 10,371,845 persons with a net loss to the South of 4,316,405.

The racial composition of the population migrating is of special significance. For the decade 1940 to 1950 the net loss of Negro persons exceeded the net loss of white persons by more than one and one-half times. Although only 53.3 per cent of white Southerners who have left their state of birth live in the non-South, 73 per cent of the Negroes have moved from the South. If present trends continue, it will be but a few years before the Negro population of the United States will be equally divided between the South and non-South.

The out-migration of Southern peoples means that the quality of public education in the South, especially that available to the Negro population, has more than academic importance for the nation as a whole and for certain selected non-Southern states in particular. In terms of race relations, the heavy exportation of Southern Negroes means that the problems of race relations which have traditionally been associated with the South become the problems of the nation, and at the same time within the South the amelioration of the problems is facilitated.

TABLE 9

Natives of South and Southern States Living in Non-Southern States by Race, 1950

[*Figures given to nearest 1,000 persons*]

	White	Negro	Total
South	4,551	2,793	7,344
Alabama	156	281	437
Arkansas	483	183	666
Florida	111	77	188
Georgia	144	349	493
Kentucky	888	95	983
Louisiana	113	170	282
Mississippi	102	332	434
N. Carolina	194	273	467
Oklahoma	711	65	777
S. Carolina	69	311	380
Tennessee	411	169	579
Texas	754	167	921
Virginia	414	322	736

SOURCE: U.S. Census of Population, 1950, Special Reports, P-E, No. 4.

THE EXPORTATION OF SOUTHERN PEOPLE

It has sometimes been said that babies are the South's most important crop. Table 10 reveals dramatic evidence of the extent to which this crop is exported to other parts of the nation and suggests how this exportation has effected the population trends of non-Southern regions.

Interstate migration has many effects, such as cultural diffusion, and in relation to education two implications are at once apparent. One is that the states receiving interstate migrants are affected proportionately by the level and quality of education in the states of origin. The other is that the same states, by furnishing education for their emigrants, have expended a proportionate amount of their effort on residents of the states to which the emigrants move. That the effects will "wash out" for a given state or region is not necessarily true.

The investments which Southern states made in the 7,344,125 persons reported in 1950 as having left the South in the decade was certainly sizable, for migration is essentially an adult affair and migrants have usually completed their schooling by the time of migration. An informed guess of the dollars and cents involved in the education of its people who left the South can be calculated by multiplying the number of migrants by a median number of years of school completed and by an average expenditure per child for these years. Such calculations yield an estimated total cost to the Southern states of two to three billion dollars. To be compared with this figure would be the cost to the other parts of the nation of educating the three million persons who migrated to the South. This investment is no doubt larger per person than the South's investment in its migrants, but it was borne by thirty-five states instead of thirteen.

TABLE 10

Effect of Cumulative Interstate Migration to 1950 by Percentage Distribution of Native Population, United States, Non-South, South, and Southern States, and Percentage Distribution of Non-Natives Living in South and Southern States by Place of Birth

	All Native Population Per Cent of Persons Born in State				Per Cent of Persons Living in State, 1950, Born in Other States		
	Living in State	Living In Other Southern States	Living In Non-South	Total	Born In Other Southern States	Born In Non-South	Total
United States....	74.4	....	....	.....	....	....	25.6
Non-South......	76.2	....	....	.....	....	....	26.0
South..........	72.4	11.3	16.3	100.0	16.1	3.9	20.0
Alabama.....	72.2	16.0	11.8	100.0	13.0	6.6	19.6
Arkansas.....	57.1	16.9	26.0	100.0	14.8	7.5	22.3
Florida.......	78.7	9.0	12.3	100.0	29.0	24.8	53.8
Georgia......	71.1	16.9	12.0	100.0	10.9	3.1	14.0
Kentucky....	67.8	6.1	26.1	100.0	5.3	6.8	12.1
Louisiana.....	78.5	11.7	9.8	100.0	11.3	3.4	14.7
Mississippi....	67.1	17.8	15.1	100.0	8.4	2.1	10.5
N. Carolina...	79.7	9.8	10.5	100.0	8.8	3.1	11.9
Oklahoma....	55.4	12.7	31.9	100.0	20.5	18.1	38.6
S. Carolina...	72.1	13.2	14.7	100.0	8.9	2.4	11.3
Tennessee....	71.4	12.7	15.9	100.0	15.5	4.1	19.6
Texas........	81.5	5.6	12.9	100.0	12.7	8.1	20.8
Virginia......	71.9	6.4	21.7	100.0	11.5	13.4	24.9

Source: U.S. Census of Population, 1950, Special Reports, P-E—No. 4.

Chapter 3

The Children of the South

SCHOOL-AGE POPULATION

The historical factors relating to the increase in population of the South come to a sharp focus in the data for school-age population. It is axiomatic that as the seedbed of the nation the South has had for many years a disportionately large percentage of its population in the school-age years.

The school-age population of the South from 1900 to 1950 increased 40 per cent. The white increase was 64 per cent, while the Negro school-age population remained constant. From 1900 to 1950 the school-age population declined from 29 per cent to 22 per cent of the total Southern population—reflecting a change from 29 to 21 per cent of the white population and 31 to 25 per cent of the Negro population.

The ratio of attendance and enrollment to school-age population has steadily increased since 1900, with the Negro rate increasing faster than the white. However, in recent years there has been little difference in the percentage of Negroes and whites of school age who are actually attending school. These increasing attendance ratios, which have come about in the South later than in other parts of the nation, have had the same effect as an equivalent increase in the school-age population. Negro changes in secondary schools have been so great as to increase percentage of attendance of school-age population from 0.5 per cent in 1900 to 28 per cent in 1940.

The decennial increases of the school-age population were checked by the depression of the 1930's. The declining birth rate during this period brought a slight decline in enrollment and attendance during the late depression years and the early part of the 1940's. However, during the decade 1940-1950, opposite trends appeared; the increasing birth rate following the depression was reflected in the increase in school population of the 6-13 age group, but the 14-17 age group decreased. By 1950 the heavy increase in birth rate during the late war and post-war years had caused the resumption of rapid growth of the school-age population.

TABLE 11

School-Age Population as a Percentage of Total Population and Attendance and Enrollment as a Percentage of School-Age Population for the South by Race, 1900-1950

	1900	1910	1920	1930	1940	1950
Total School Population						
School-Age Population as a Percentage of Total Population.	29.4	28.9	29.1	28.0	24.6	21.7
Enrollment as Percentage of Total School-Age Population.	70.8	77.3	83.8	89.5	93.6	92.9
Attendance as a Percentage of Total School-Age Population.	46.6	50.0	58.3	68.7	77.4	80.3
White School Population						
School-Age Population as a Percentage of Total White Population.	29.0	28.2	28.8	27.7	24.0	20.8
Enrollment as Percentage of White School-Age Population.	76.4	83.1	87.2	91.5	94.3	92.8
Attendance as a Percentage of White School-Age Population.	51.5	54.4	61.5	71.5	79.0	80.7
Negro School Population						
School-Age Population as a Percentage of Total Negro Population.	31.2	30.2	30.0	28.9	25.5	25.0
Enrollment as Percentage of Negro School-Age Population.	59.3	65.7	75.7	84.1	91.7	93.4
Attendance as a Percentage of Negro School-Age Population.	36.9	41.3	50.8	61.3	73.4	79.3

SOURCE: White and Negro population data from U.S. Census of Population, 1950, and *Negroes in the United States 1920-32*.

SCHOOL-AGE POPULATION BY AGE GROUPS

School-age population is usually a reflection of the total population and, like total population, it varies significantly from state to state in the South and from age group to age group.

The average school-age population per state is 764,000. Eight of the states fall below this average and five lie above it. The largest number is found in Texas, with a total for the two age groups of 1,700,000, or over 19 per cent of the total school-age population in the South. Arkansas with a total of 485,000 has the smallest school-age population, less than 5 per cent of the total. The large population of a few states tends to throw the average away from the median state, Kentucky, with a school-age population of 716,000. Obviously, the largest population is found in the 5-13 age group, corresponding to the elementary plus kindergarten grades. Because there is still a small number of kindergarten or nursery school grades in the South, the age 5 is usually excluded from the censuses of school-age population. But as the advance of Southern public school education continues, a steady rise of these grades is anticipated. Therefore, age 5 is included in this table and later is projected into the future school-age population of the South. (See Chapter 6.)

Of special interest is the state-by-state variation of Negro 5-17 population. Only in Mississippi does the traditional fifty-fifty distribution of white and Negro still hold; there, in fact, in 1950 Negro exceeded white school-age population a fraction. The Negro school population as percentages of the state totals in 1950 were: Alabama, 35; Arkansas, 24; Florida, 25; Georgia, 35; Kentucky, 6; Louisiana, 37; Mississippi, 51; North Carolina, 31; Oklahoma, 10; South Carolina, 46; Tennessee, 16; Texas, 14; and Virginia, 25. The range is thus from 6 per cent in Kentucky to 51 per cent in Mississippi. The regional percentage is 26, which is approximately the median percentage for the states; hence, the distribution lies fairly evenly above and below the middle point.

The states with the higher ratios are as a rule those which are faced with the largest task of equalization of expenditures by race. The other states will in all probability achieve racial equalization somewhat earlier than these. Moreover, it is the states with large Negro total school-age population ratios which must do most to achieve equalization of expenditures irrespective of race—here termed "across-the-board" equalization.

[37]

TABLE 12

School-Age Population by Age Groups, 5-13, 14-17, in South and Southern States by Race, 1950

[*Figures given to nearest 1,000 persons*]

	WHITE		NEGRO		TOTAL		Total School-Age Population
	5-13	14-17	5-13	14-17	5-13	14-17	
South..........	5,311	2,047	1,860	712	7,171	2,760	9,931
Alabama......	371*	144*	200	78	571	223	794
Arkansas.....	266	103	84	32	350	135	485
Florida.......	301	107	99	37	400	144	544
Georgia.......	395	154	213	82	608	236	844
Kentucky.....	482	191	30	13	512*	204	716*
Louisiana.....	299	108	174	64*	473	172	645
Mississippi....	204	80	213	80	417	160	577
N. Carolina...	508	206	227	87	735	293	1,028
Oklahoma.....	325	132	38	15	363	147	510
S. Carolina....	224	88	192	71	416	159	575
Tennessee.....	467	183	88	35	555	218	773
Texas.........	1,065	402	167*	66	1,232	468	1,700
Virginia......	404	149	135	52	539	201*	740

SOURCE: U.S. Census of Population, 1950.
*The median state for each category.

ENROLLMENT BY RACE

The decline in total enrollment in the South was reversed in 1951-52, with a gain since 1939-40 of 2.2 per cent. The total enrollment reached in 1951-52 was 8,667,728, the largest in the history of the South.

Table 13 depicts the developments. Consider first the changes in elementary enrollment. From 1939-40 through 1951-52, eight of the Southern states experienced increases in white elementary enrollment. The largest increases were recorded by Florida, Texas, and South Carolina. Five states showed declines for both races and eleven for Negro children. The greatest drops in white enrollment took place in Oklahoma, Mississippi, and Arkansas. Oklahoma, Kentucky, Arkansas, and Mississippi showed decreases in Negro elementary enrollment. Only two states, Florida and Louisiana, can claim increases for both races in elementary enrollment.

The net effect for the region in elementary enrollment has been an increase of 5.0 per cent in white, a decrease of 6.9 per cent in Negro, making an aggregate increase for both races of 1.4 per cent.

Consider the changes in secondary enrollment. The advances in this category continued to be significant. Seven states—Arkansas, Florida, Georgia, Kentucky, Oklahoma, Tennessee, and Virginia— show increases in secondary enrollment for both races, with the greatest for the Negro children. The growth in this period continued a long-range trend. Between 1900 and 1950, overall secondary enrollment increased 2,839 per cent, with the Negro high school enrollment rising from 3,412 in 1900 to 317,600 in 1950—an increase of 9,208 per cent!

The rise in secondary enrollment of white children is not nearly as significant; the largest growth is Florida's 30.4 per cent and the next largest, Georgia's 16.2 per cent. Not a single state records a decrease in Negro secondary enrollment; but Louisiana, Mississippi, North Carolina, Oklahoma, South Carolina, and Texas all record decreases in white secondary enrollment.

The net effect for the region in secondary enrollment is a 2.8 per cent decrease in white, a 54.7 per cent increase in Negro, and a 5.1 per cent increase for both races.

Total enrollment for both races for the region has increased 2.2 per cent over the period 1939-40 through 1951-52. Total white enrollment, elementary plus secondary, has increased 3.2 per cent. Total Negro enrollment, elementary plus secondary, has decreased but 0.7 per cent.

These trends reflect various developments. The reversal in overall enrollment is accounted for by such factors as the impact of the rapid rise in the birth rate during and after World War II, increasing urbanization, and the expanding economy. The great increases in Negro secondary enrollment probably reflect the latter development more than any other. For those states in which losses in enrollment are recorded, out-migration has been significant. This process appears to be coming to a halt as the South improves its economic position; and by the end of the 1950's in-migrants may balance or exceed out-migrants. In any case, the reversal in overall enrollment to an upward trend foretells the educational problems to come.

TABLE 13
Elementary and Secondary Enrollment and Percentage Change in South and Southern States by Race, 1939-40 to 1951-52
[Figures given to nearest 1,000 pupils]

	1939-40			1951-52			PERCENTAGE CHANGE FROM 1939-40 TO 1951-52		
	Elementary	Secondary	Total	Elementary	Secondary	Total	Elementary	Secondary	Total
South									
Total	6,811	1,674	8,486	6,908	1,759	8,668	1.4	4.5	2.2
White	4,788	1,446	6,235	5,025	1,406	6,432	5.0	− 2.8	3.2
Negro	2,023	228	2,251	1,883	353	2,236	− 6.9	54.7	− 0.7
Alabama									
Total	586	100	687	547	132	679	− 6.7	31.6	− 1.1
White	364	83	447	346	93	440	− 4.8	12.4	− 1.6
Negro	222	17	240	201	39	239	− 9.7	124.4	− 0.1
Arkansas									
Total	398	74	472	334	82	416	−16.1	10.8	−11.8
White	291	66	357	248	69	316	−14.8	3.4	−11.4
Negro	108	7	115	87	14	100	−19.6	84.4	−13.0
Florida									
Total	306	81	387	424	112	536	39.8	38.3	38.4
White	214	69	283	318	90	408	48.8	30.4	44.3
Negro	93	11	104	106	21	127	14.4	86.2	22.3
Georgia									
Total	602	132	734	570	174	744	− 5.3	31.6	1.3
White	358	111	469	360	129	490	0.8	16.2	4.4
Negro	245	21	266	210	44	254	−14.2	113.8	− 4.2
Kentucky									
Total	511	98	609	462	99	561	− 9.5	1.3	− 7.8
White	473	91	564	433	93	526	− 8.4	1.4	− 6.9
Negro	37	7	44	29	7	35	−23.3	0.9	−19.6
Louisiana									
Total	368	101	469	413	95	508	12.3	− 5.8	8.2
White	211	84	295	243	68	312	15.5	−18.9	5.7
Negro	157	17	175	170	27	197	8.1	52.4	12.5
Mississippi									
Total	524	74	599	449	86	535	−14.3	16.1	−10.6
White	242	63	306	206	62	268	−15.2	− 2.3	−12.5
Negro	282	11	293	244	24	268	−13.6	123.7	− 8.5
N. Carolina									
Total	688	203	891	720	190	910	4.7	− 6.5	2.1
White	456	163	620	494	142	637	8.3	−13.0	2.7
Negro	231	40	271	226	48	273	− 2.5	20.4	0.9
Oklahoma									
Total	467	139	605	380	120	500	−18.5	−13.8	−17.4
White	427	131	558	352	112	464	−17.5	−14.9	−16.9
Negro	39	8	47	28	8	36	−29.0	5.2	−23.4
S. Carolina									
Total	395	87	482	426	86	512	8.0	− 1.3	6.3
White	196	70	266	228	57	285	16.2	−18.7	7.0
Negro	199	17	216	198	29	228	− 0.1	69.2	5.4
Tennessee									
Total	535	108	643	547	130	677	2.2	20.0	5.2
White	440	95	535	456	110	566	3.7	15.3	5.8
Negro	95	13	108	91	20	111	− 4.7	55.1	2.5
Texas									
Total	990	347	1,336	1,158	298	1,456	16.0	−14.1	9.0
White	804	310	1,114	990	260	1,249	23.1	−16.1	12.2
Negro	185	37	223	169	38	207	− 9.1	2.6	− 7.2
Virginia									
Total	441	131	572	476	157	633	8.0	20.1	10.8
White	312	109	421	350	122	473	12.2	12.5	12.3
Negro	129	22	151	126	34	160	− 2.3	58.0	6.5

AVERAGE DAILY ATTENDANCE

Average daily attendance—the average number of students present each school day—has shown a sizable increase for the South over the years. But on a state-by-state basis there has been considerable variability.

Table 14 brings together the attendance data by state and by race for the school years 1939-40 and 1951-52. The majority of the Southern states show an increase in ADA. For the region as a whole, the attendance of white children increased 6.9 per cent and the attendance of Negro children, 5.6 per cent.

The largest increase over this span of years developed in Florida: 44.1 per cent for white and 29.3 per cent for Negro children. Arkansas, Kentucky, and Oklahoma register decreases; the most significant is Oklahoma's 16.6 per cent decrease for the white and 15.4 per cent decrease for the Negro children.

As educational and health programs in the South are expanded and as Southern families achieve greater economic security, more and more children are able to attend school regularly. Even though school-age population has grown only about 40 per cent since 1900, public school attendance has risen by 134.7 per cent.

The increase in ADA has been more pronounced in rural and rural-urban counties than in metropolitan areas. In 1940, ADA, as a percentage of enrollment, in rural and rural-urban counties stood at 81.2 and 81.9 per cent, respectively. By 1952 these percentages had increased to 85.3 for rural and 84.9 for rural-urban. This reflects the recent emphasis on state-wide minimum foundation programs, which have spurred rural and rural-urban school improvement. In the metropolitan areas where the school systems were already fairly well developed, attendance showed less growth—from the 1940 percentage of 84.7 to the 1952 percentage of 86.2.

TABLE 14

Average Daily Attendance in Public Schools of South and Southern States by Race, 1939-40 and 1951-52

	1939-40		1951-52		Percentage Change 1939-40 and 1951-52	
	White	Negro	White	Negro	White	Negro
South	5,221,782	1,800,351	5,580,450	1,902,001	6.9	5.6
Alabama	370,033	196,640	383,679	203,716	3.7	3.6
Arkansas	284,274	89,082	268,235	82,617	− 5.7	− 7.3
Florida	238,960	87,031	344,319	112,524	44.1	29.3
Georgia	381,295	202,580	429,951	207,578	12.8	2.5
Kentucky	457,793	35,417	446,909	30,696	− 2.4	−13.3
Louisiana	253,722	144,392	276,662	169,048	9.0	17.1
Mississippi	247,251	226,769	244,605	226,864	− 1.1	0.0
N. Carolina	559,779	230,224	576,117	239,919	2.9	4.2
Oklahoma	447,434	37,462	373,083	31,684	−16.6	−15.4
S. Carolina	222,800	162,195	244,889	182,437	9.9	12.5
Tennessee	446,766	89,949	496,574	97,946	11.1	8.9
Texas	943,419	172,844	1,079,063	176,534	14.4	2.1
Virginia	368,256	125,766	416,364	140,438	13.1	11.7

ENROLLMENT AND ATTENDANCE BY PLACE OF RESIDENCE

Tables 15 and 16 point up the significant changes in school-age enrollment and attendance wrought by the drift towards rurbanization. Enrollment has decreased in both rural and rural-urban counties while it has risen markedly in metropolitan counties. The drop for the period 1940 through 1952 in the rural population is 7.5 per cent and for rural-urban, 4.8 per cent. But the metropolitan counties, as Table 16 shows, have experienced an increase, 26.8 per cent.

The changes in enrollment generate changes throughout the region in average daily attendance. Rurbanization fosters a higher attendance ratio than has been the pattern in the predominantly agrarian South of the past. During the dozen years intervening between the 1940 census and the year 1952, attendance as a percentage of enrollment advanced somewhat more in the metropolitan counties than it did in the rural and rural-urban counties. Table 15 portrays quite clearly the patterns now in development. It is well known that school attendance has for decades been relatively greater in the city than in the country. However, the influence of the metropolitan school practices is spreading.

Equalization in attendance by race is also in prospect. During the same period, Negro school attendance in rural areas rose from 78.6 per cent to 84.1 per cent. While this increase lags behind that in the metropolitan schools, the gap is fairly narrow, some 3.6 per cent. Of considerable interest is the greater attendance of Negro compared to white children in metropolitan counties, probably a temporary variation, however. In 1940 the Negro and white attendance to enrollment percentages were 85.5 and 82.5, respectively. But in 1952 the Negro position is reversed and the white percentage of 85.6 lies below the Negro percentage of 87.7. Here, too, improvements in education are operating positively.

There is, of course, a limit to which attendance may rise, and the present ratios may be close to that limit.

TABLE 15

Attendance as a Percentage of Enrollment in Public Schools of Sample Rural and Rural-Urban Counties and of Metropolitan Counties in Thirteen Southern States by Race, 1939-40, 1949-50, and 1951-52

County Classification	1939-40			1949-50			1951-52		
	White	Negro	Total	White	Negro	Total	White	Negro	Total
Rural.............	82.5	78.6	81.2	86.2	83.8	85.3	86.0	84.1	85.3
Rural-Urban........	83.1	79.3	81.9	86.6	84.0	85.7	86.2	82.0	84.9
Metropolitan........	85.5	82.5	84.7	87.2	88.1	87.4	85.6	87.7	86.2

TABLE 16

Changes in Enrollment in Sample Rural and Rural-Urban Counties, and in Metropolitan Counties of Thirteen Southern States by Race, 1939-40 to 1951-52

County Classification	PERCENTAGE CHANGE	
	1939-40	1951-52
Rural.........................	−7.5	−7.5
Rural-Urban...................	−5.5	−4.8
Metropolitan...................	15.7	26.8

Chapter 4

Some Qualitative Measures of Southern Schooling

THE MEDIAN YEAR OF SCHOOL COMPLETED

One measure of the educational profile of a population is the median year of school completed. In Tables 17 and 18, 1950 data are drawn from the median state in each region as representative.

Generally, for all parts of the nation, the number of years of schooling increased steadily up to about age 19; persons between ages 20 and 29 reported an average scarcely higher than the 19-year-old group. Among the population of the nation as a whole above the age level 13, male educational attainment lags behind female, although the differences are slight. This is true of the South and of the North and West, as well as for the total United States.

As respects older age brackets, white males aged 45 and over had about as much schooling as the 14- and 15-year-olds, and those 65 and older slightly more than 13-year-olds. Both sexes among whites showed less than the ninth year completed at all age levels above 55. Regional differences in the older ages were comparatively slight.

For the nation, the white population 20 to 29 showed a median school completion past high school for both sexes, but in the South the attainment was significantly lower.

In the ages between 14 and 19, a difference of about one year separated the South from the North and West for the white males and a little less for the females. Place of residence is a governing factor in terms of the number of years of school completed since urban dwellers tend to remain in school longer than rural. The Southern deficiency is larger among the older segment of the 14-19 group, reflecting the higher proportion of rural population in the region.

As seen in Table 18, the non-white differences in the nation are minor for the 5-13 age group. The racial contrast becomes marked at age 14 and increases with the rise in age levels. At 14 and 15 years, the non-white males were 1.5 years behind the white group, and the non-white females were 1.1 years behind. The 18- to 19-year-old non-white males had 2.8 years less schooling than the white, and the non-white females, 2.2 years less than the white. The differential between Southern non-white and Southern white at 18 and 19 is 2.7 years for males and 2.0 years for females. While the Southern non-

TABLE 17

Median School Years Completed for Whites in United States,
North and West, and South by Sex

Age	UNITED STATES		NORTH AND WEST		SOUTH	
	Male	Female	Male	Female	Male	Female
5*............	Under 1.0	Under 1.0	Under 1.0	Under 1.0	Under 1.0	Under 1.0
6.............	1.5	1.5	1.5	1.5	1.5	1.5
7.............	2.2	2.2	2.3	2.3	2.0	2.0
8.............	3.1	3.1	3.2	3.2	2.9	2.9
9.............	4.1	4.1	4.2	4.2	3.8	3.8
10............	5.0	5.0	5.1	5.1	4.7	4.7
11............	6.0	6.0	6.1	6.1	5.7	5.7
12............	6.9	6.9	7.0	7.0	6.6	6.6
13............	7.9	7.9	8.0	8.0	7.5	7.5
14-15.........	8.2	8.5	8.4	8.6	7.6	8.2
16-17.........	9.0	10.2	10.2	10.4	9.4	9.9
18-19.........	11.5	12.1	11.9	12.2	10.6	11.3
20-21.........	12.2	12.3	12.3	12.4	11.3	12.0
22-24.........	12.2	12.2	12.2	12.3	10.9	11.7
25-29.........	12.1	12.2	12.2	12.3	11.0	11.5
30-34.........	11.9	12.1	12.1	12.1	10.4	10.8
35-44.........	10.4	11.0	10.8	11.4	9.1	10.1
45-54.........	8.8	9.0	8.9	9.2	8.5	8.9
55-64.........	8.4	8.6	8.5	8.6	8.1	8.4
65-74.........	8.2	8.4	8.3	8.5	7.4	8.1
75 and Over....	8.1	8.3	8.2	8.4	6.9	7.8

SOURCE: U.S. Census of Population, 1950.
*Median school years for children 5-13 are given as the year in which the child is enrolled.

whites at these ages were below the level of the ninth grade in their schooling, the white national norm stood approximately at completion of high school and the white Southern level was nearing completion of high school.

The most significant implication of the non-white figures emerges from a comparison of the education levels of the older age groups. The 55-64 non-white males in the South had almost the same attainment as the Southern 10-year-old non-white males and females. Thus grandparents and their younger grandchildren had about the same educational status.

The Southern non-white males between the ages of 30 and 55 had six or less years of schooling placing them at the level of their 12-year-old children. They had approximately 2.6 years less schooling than non-white males residing in the North and West, many of whom are Southern migrants; this suggests an educational differential in emigration from the South.

It would appear inescapable that the relatively low educational attainment of the non-white population of parental and grandparental age constitutes a handicap for the school-age population since much learning takes place in the home. When it is observed that the educational attainment of the white population of the parental and grandparental ages is more than twice that of the non-white, the racial handicap is clear.

TABLE 18

Median School Years Completed for Non-Whites for United States, North and West, and South by Sex

Age	UNITED STATES		NORTH AND WEST		SOUTH	
	Male	Female	Male	Female	Male	Female
5*..........	Under 1.0	Under 1.0	Under 1.0	Under 1.0	Under 1.0	Under 1.0
6............	1.5	1.5	1.6	1.6	1.5	1.5
7............	2.0	2.0	2.3	2.3	1.4	1.9
8............	2.8	2.8	3.2	3.2	2.6	2.6
9............	3.6	3.6	4.0	4.0	3.4	3.4
10...........	4.4	4.4	5.0	5.0	4.1	4.1
11...........	5.2	5.2	5.8	5.8	5.0	5.0
12...........	6.1	6.1	6.7	6.7	6.7	6.7
13...........	6.9	6.9	7.7	7.7	6.5	6.5
14-15........	6.7	7.4	7.9	8.4	6.3	7.1
16-17........	8.2	9.2	9.7	10.0	7.4	8.8
18-19........	8.7	9.9	10.5	11.1	7.9	9.3
20-21........	8.8	9.9	10.6	11.3	7.8	9.1
22-24........	8.6	9.6	10.4	11.1	7.5	8.6
25-29........	8.3	8.9	10.2	10.7	7.0	7.9
30-34........	7.8	8.4	9.4	9.8	6.5	7.4
35-44........	6.8	7.5	8.4	8.7	5.7	6.7
45-54........	5.8	6.5	7.4	7.8	4.8	5.8
55-64........	4.9	5.6	6.7	7.0	4.1	4.9
65-74........	3.9	4.3	5.8	6.0	3.3	3.8
75 and Over....	2.9	3.2	4.4	4.9	2.5	2.8

SOURCE: U.S. Census of Population, 1950.
*Median School Years for Children 5-13 are given as the year in which the child is enrolled.

THE PUPIL LOAD PER TEACHER

In earlier decades of public education in the South the number of pupils in ADA per teacher was frequently sizable, sometimes as much as 40 or more. The Negro school teacher as a rule was more burdened than the white teacher.

Table 19 gives evidence of a noticeable change for the better. By 1940 in Southern elementary schools the white teacher had an average of 28 pupils under her wing and the Negro teacher 33 pupils. In secondary schools, white classes averaged 22 and Negro classes 24.

By 1952 the gap of 5 in elementary schools had narrowed to about 2, but the gap in the secondary schools had risen by one. These differences probably reflect year-by-year variations; for all intents and purposes, the average size of the Negro classes approaches the white average.

There are of course variations among the states. Some states still have a fairly large gap. Others have equalized the classroom burdens of Negro and white teachers, and two—Oklahoma and Virginia—have larger white classes than Negro classes at the elementary level.

A review of Table 20 reveals no obvious pattern in size of class by county classification. If anything, the classrooms in metropolitan areas have tended to run somewhat higher than in rural and rural-urban areas—a reflection, no doubt, of the trend toward urbanization.

By 1951-52, equalization in the secondary schools of the classroom size was essentially achieved. However, the elementary schools in the cities still had an average of 4 more Negro than white pupils per classroom.

[49]

TABLE 19

Number of Pupils in Average Daily Attendance per Classroom Teacher in Public Elementary and Secondary Schools of Twelve Southern States by Race, 1939-40 and 1951-52

	1939-40				1951-52			
	Elementary		Secondary		Elementary		Secondary	
	White	Negro	White	Negro	White	Negro	White	Negro
The Twelve States..	28.2	32.7	21.7	23.8	29.1	30.6	18.2	20.5
Alabama.......	28.3	36.8	24.4	28.2	28.2	28.9	22.7	24.1
Arkansas.......	31.5	38.3	18.7	15.3	35.7	39.1	13.5	12.9
Florida........	24.1	27.6	25.4	25.6	25.8	26.6	22.5	22.2
Georgia........	26.7	31.6	17.7	17.8	26.6	28.5	19.5	19.7
Kentucky......	28.6	26.3	22.7	21.7	28.2	27.4	22.1	19.6
Louisiana.......	26.4	36.3	18.9	25.7	27.7	33.3	13.5	16.4
Mississippi.....	36.6	38.7	22.3	14.1	34.0	37.4	14.9	18.3
N. Carolina.....	33.5	33.2	28.3	31.6	30.1	31.8	22.5	26.0
Oklahoma......	25.2	22.0	18.8	19.2	31.1	29.1	14.6	14.7
S. Carolina.....	25.1	29.1	20.6	25.4	26.1	26.2	19.5	23.2
Texas..........	26.2	29.2	21.1	24.0	28.9	26.5	15.8	17.9
Virginia........	30.2	32.0	21.9	23.3	30.6	34.2	18.5	20.3

TABLE 20

Number of Pupils in Average Daily Attendance per Classroom Teacher in Public Elementary and Secondary Schools in Sample Rural and Rural-Urban Counties, and in Metropolitan Counties of Eight Southern States by Race, 1939-40 and 1951-52

	1939-40				1951-52			
	Elementary		Secondary		Elementary		Secondary	
	White	Negro	White	Negro	White	Negro	White	Negro
Rural............	27.4	32.9	21.4	23.3	29.7	30.5	17.8	20.6
Rural-Urban.......	28.7	33.2	22.2	24.3	28.3	30.6	19.7	21.1
Metropolitan......	29.1	36.3	24.5	28.8	27.9	32.0	20.7	22.3

TRAINING COMPLETED BY SOUTHERN TEACHERS

The amount of training of public school teachers is shown here by the number of years of college education received; this is not necessarily a measure of teaching skill, but it provides at least a formal comparison by periods and by race.

As late as 1930, there were many classes, Negro and white, conducted by teachers with no college training and in some cases no high school diploma. Even by 1939-40, there were substantial differences in the training of teachers of the two races. Some 30 per cent of Negro teachers had less than two years of college as compared to 6.5 per cent of white teachers. Only 35.5 per cent of Negro teachers in that year had four or more years of training as against 61 per cent of white teachers. By 1952 the gap in training had been almost closed. For the region as a whole, there is now only a fraction of a year's difference in the average schooling of the Negro and white teacher.

Not all states have narrowed this gap to the same degree, of course. In Mississippi, for example, the percentage of white teachers with four years or more of training for the year 1951-52 is about twice the number of Negro teachers. In six states, Georgia, North Carolina, Oklahoma, Tennessee, Texas, and Virginia, the training of Negro teachers on the average exceeded the training of white teachers. In Georgia and Oklahoma, there are few Negro teachers with less than two years of college. This relatively high level of qualification mirrors the esteem in which teaching as a profession is held in Negro communities, as well as the improvement in the lot of Negro teachers in public schools.

TABLE 21

Percentage of White and Negro Teachers with Specified Years of Training for Ten Southern States, 1939-40, 1949-50, 1951-52

Years of Training	White Teachers			Negro Teachers		
	1939-40	1949-50	1951-52	1939-40	1949-50	1951-52
Less than Two	6.5	6.0	3.3	29.7	13.5	9.0
Two or Three	32.5	21.5	18.5	34.8	20.5	17.7
Four or More	61.0	72.5	78.2	35.5	66.0	73.3
Total	100.0	100.0	100.0	100.0	100.0	100.0

LENGTH OF SCHOOL TERM

One aspect of improvement in Southern public education is the increasing length of the school term. As late as 1939-40, the average length of the school term for white pupils in the South was 169 days as compared with 153 days for Negro pupils. But by 1951-52, the gap had narrowed to only one day—177 for white children and 176 for Negro children.

In a number of states school terms of 179 or 180 days for both Negro and white pupils were mandatory. Only two states—Arkansas and Mississippi—fell noticeably below the average.

The upward trend has been maintained in rural counties as well as in metropolitan areas. In 1939-40 the average length in days for white pupils in rural schools was 165; for Negro pupils, 147. In 1951-52, the rural figures were 177 for white pupils and 175 for Negro pupils.

Metropolitan schools required white pupils to attend 175 days in 1939-40; Negro pupils, 168 days. Both groups of children were required to attend 179 days on the average in the South in 1951-52.

TABLE 22

Average Length in Days of the School Term in Public Schools in Twelve Southern States by Race, 1939-40, 1949-50, 1951-52

	1939-40		1949-50		1951-52	
	White	Negro	White	Negro	White	Negro
The Twelve States	169	153	177	173	177	176
Alabama	157	147	176	177	176	176
Arkansas	163	144	175	169	172	171
Florida	169	164	180	180	180	180
Georgia	170	135	180	176	180	180
Kentucky	166	159	179	177	179	179
Louisiana	180	144	180	171	179	174
Mississippi	160	124	160	141	167	158
N. Carolina	164	164	180	180	180	180
S. Carolina	175	147	180	174	180	178
Tennessee	164	162	176	176	176	176
Texas	174	162	176	176	176	176
Virginia	180	180	180	180	180	180

TABLE 23

Average Length in Days of the School Term in Public Schools in Sample Rural and Rural-Urban Counties, and in Metropolitan Counties in Twelve Southern States by Race, 1939-40, 1949-50, and 1951-52

County Classification	1939-40		1949-50		1951-52	
	White	Negro	White	Negro	White	Negro
Rural	165	147	177	172	177	175
Rural-Urban	169	154	177	175	177	176
Metropolitan	175	168	179	179	179	179

PUBLIC SCHOOL LIBRARIES

The South had made very little progress before the 1940's in assembling much-needed libraries. Seven Southern states for which data are available averaged 2.3 books per pupil in 1939-40. By 1951-52 there had been an increase of 1.1 books per pupil to 3.4 books per pupil, or a 48 per cent change. (See Table 24.) Negro pupils had but 0.7 of a book per pupil in 1939-40, while white pupils averaged 2.9 books per pupil. In 1952 the Negro schools had reached 2.0 books per pupil and the white schools 4.3 books per pupil—still far from equalization. Obviously, either average is still well below the desirable standard of an adequate school library.

Metropolitan counties on the whole have fared better than rural and rural-urban counties in library accumulation. Yet in the metropolitan schools, as of 1951-52, libraries for Negro pupils had not attained equality with libraries for white pupils in the average number of volumes per pupil.

Although the data are incomplete, trends in public school library expenditures per pupil may be derived from Table 25. In current dollars, expenditures have more than doubled for the states as a group, with expenditures per pupil in 1939-40 of 29 cents and in 1951-52 of 75 cents. However, if consideration is given to the fact that the prices of books and periodicals have approximately doubled, then little more was being spent on libraries in 1951-52 than a dozen years earlier.

TABLE 24
Library Books per Pupil in ADA, in Southern States, 1939-40 to 1951-52

	Library Volumes Per Pupil Enrolled			Change Per Pupil 1940-1952	
	1939-40	1949-50	1951-52	Number	Per Cent
State Totals					
7 States Total	2.3	3.8	3.4	1.1	48
White	2.9	4.6	4.3	1.4	48
Negro	0.7	1.7	2.0	1.3	186
Rural County Sample					
10 States Total	2.1	3.6	3.4	1.3	62
White	2.8	4.9	4.5	1.7	61
Negro	0.6	1.4	1.6	1.0	167
Rural-Urban County Sample					
10 States Total	2.1	2.9	3.3	1.2	57
White	2.7	4.4	4.2	1.5	56
Negro	0.8	1.5	2.0	1.2	150
Metropolitan Counties					
10 States Total	2.1	3.5	3.5	1.4	67
White	2.5	3.9	4.0	1.5	60
Negro	0.8	2.2	2.4	1.6	200

TABLE 25
Library Expenditures per Pupil in Southern States, 1939-40 to 1951-52

	Library Expenditures Per Pupil in Average Daily Attendance			Change Per Pupil 1940-1950	
	1939-40	1949-50	1951-52	Amount	Per Cent
State Totals					
9 States Total	$0.24	$0.62	$0.75	$0.51	212
White*	0.29	0.45	0.86	0.57	197
Negro	0.09	0.21	0.66	0.57	633
Rural County Sample					
9 States Total	0.28	0.49	0.67	0.39	139
White	0.36	0.56	0.68	0.32	89
Negro	0.09	0.38	0.66	0.57	633
Rural-Urban County Sample					
9 States Total	0.26	0.51	0.76	0.50	192
White	0.33	0.58	0.85	0.52	158
Negro	0.08	0.33	0.56	0.48	600
Metropolitan Counties					
9 States Total	0.34	1.05	1.01	0.67	197
White	0.40	1.03	0.98	0.58	145
Negro	0.18	1.10	1.12	0.94	522

*The white total is 7 states.

VOCATIONAL EDUCATION

Vocational programs are concerned with four occupational areas: agriculture, home economics, trades and industries, and distributive occupations. In the South the greatest number of pupils, 212 per thousand, are enrolled in home economics, with an enrollment of 130 per thousand in agriculture; trades and industries are third in rank; and distributive trades are still of relatively minor importance, to judge by a very small enrollment of 6 per thousand for all the Southern states.

The cost of the programs varies considerably, as may be seen in Table 26. Distributive occupations involve so far the highest outlay; for example, in 1951-52, $117.09 per white pupil, compared to $85.46 per white pupil and $46.75 per white pupil in agriculture and trades and industries. The least costly program is home economics, $42.08.

The rise in outlays from 1939-40 to 1951-52 is relatively great. For example, in agriculture the outlays for all the states on white pupils increased 102.5 per cent; in home economics, 129.7 per cent; in trades and industries, 106.6 per cent; and in distributive occupations, 42.4 per cent. The increases in outlays tended to be somewhat less in metropolitan counties than they were in other counties, to judge by the samples available. That these increases are educationally significant is quite debatable, for a very large portion of them can be accounted for by the rise in prices of materials and machines and other costs.

Of particular interest is the tendency to spend more on Negro pupils than on white pupils in trades and industries and distributive occupations for the states as a group and for metropolitan counties. On the other hand more is spent on white pupils in agriculture and home economics. This difference is partly attributable to change taking place in the Southern economy and the concomitant movement of Negroes into trades and industries and distributive occupations in recent years.

TABLE 26
Expenditures per Pupil Enrolled in Vocational Education in Public High Schools of Southern States by Race, 1939-40 and 1951-52, and Negro Expenditures as Percentage of White for 1951-52

	1939-40		1951-52		Negro Expenditure as Percentage of White 1951-52
	White	Negro	White	Negro	
State Totals					
Agriculture*.............	$42.20	$27.27	$85.46	$65.24	76.3
Home Economics*.........	18.33	8.21	42.08	32.64	77.6
Trades and Industries†.....	22.63	13.31	46.75	51.92	111.1
Distributive Occupations‡..	82.24	n.e.§	117.09	163.11	139.3
Rural County Sample					
Agriculture*.............	51.98	26.34	91.69	62.47	68.1
Home Economics‡.........	20.68	9.96	49.26	39.64	80.5
Trades and Industries*.....	32.10	n.e.	83.40	58.90	70.6
Distributive Occupations‡..	n.e.	n.e.	82.35	n.e.	....
Rural-Urban County Sample					
Agriculture*.............	47.30	19.98	83.57	38.13	45.6
Home Economics‡.........	19.27	8.63	44.28	29.92	67.6
Trades and Industries*.....	25.00	10.59	49.79	48.56	97.5
Distributive Occupations‡..	105.55	n.e.	107.77	n.e.	....
Metropolitan Counties					
Agriculture*.............	48.63	27.85	82.58	59.05	71.5
Home Economics‡.........	15.00	6.22	37.74	34.76	92.1
Trades and Industries*.....	20.41	14.58	50.11	54.07	107.9
Distributive Occupations‡..	78.30	n.e.	118.09	125.96	106.7

*7 states. †6 states. ‡10 states. ‡8 states. §None enrolled.

TABLE 27
Pupils Enrolled in Vocational Programs per Thousand Pupils in High Schools of Southern States by Race, 1939-40 and 1951-52, and the Negro Enrollment as a Percentage of White, 1951-52

	1939-40		1951-52		Negro Expenditure as Percentage of White 1951-52
	White	Negro	White	Negro	
State Totals					
Agriculture*............	92	126	135	117	87.7
Home Economics†.........	128	210	202	252	124.7
Trades and Industries‡.....	43	85	83	74	89.2
Distributive Occupations‡..	1	0	7	1	14.3

*12 States. †12 States. ‡7 States. ‡12 States.

TEACHERS' SALARIES

Before the 1940's, the differences between salaries of white and Negro teachers in the South were less a measure of qualification that of official discrimination. Individual variations in training, tenure, and experience have persisted but, as more money has become available for education, and as school equalization has progressed, the salaries of Negro teachers have closely approached those of white teachers similarly qualified. One or two states, in fact, are paying more on the average to Negroes than to whites.

Tables 28 and 29 show the development of this trend between 1939-40 and 1951-52. The data are all in terms of 1935-1939 dollars, so that the inflationary effects are removed and meaningful comparisons are made possible.

For the twelve Southern states reporting, from 1939-40 to 1951-52, the average annual salary of white teachers rose from $962 to $1,460, an increase of 51.8 per cent. In the same period, the average annual salaries of Negro teachers advanced three times as much—from $505 to $1,273, an increase of 152.1 per cent. The largest efforts, percentagewise, have been made by Louisiana; there, in 1939-40 the average "real" salary per Negro teacher was $391, but by 1951-52 it had reached $1,420, an increase of 263.2 per cent. This average, however, is still less than the average for the white teachers. In Arkansas, Mississippi, and Tennessee, the average salaries for both white and Negro teachers lie significantly below the average for the region. As will be seen, these states face the greatest problems in achieving overall equalization of expenditures.

North Carolina, Oklahoma, Tennessee, and Virginia have not only equalized white and Negro teachers' salaries, but on the average are actually paying Negro teachers more than white teachers. The states at the door of equalization are Alabama, Florida, Georgia, Louisiana, and Texas.

Teachers in the rural counties receive lower "real" salaries than do teachers in rural-urban and metropolitan counties. These differences may be partly determined by relative training and experience. The highly trained teachers and those with experience tend to gravitate towards the populous areas where, as a rule, salaries are higher than in the rural counties. In each of these region-wide classifications, the Negro teachers receive lower salaries than white teachers. By 1951-52, however, the gaps between the teachers of the two races had shrunk considerably.

Teachers in the South generally have not fared nearly as well as they might have in business or government. And workers with far less education than most public school teachers have fared much better. In 1939-40, workers engaged in manufacturing industries in the United States on the average received adjusted annual wages of $1,278, as compared to the average salary for all teachers in the South—$851—or to the average salary of white teachers —$962. In 1951-52, the workers earned $1,838, the average wage adjusted for price level changes, as compared to the average salary of white teachers of $1,460 and $1,273 for Negro teachers, also adjusted. One further comparison should be made. From Stephen Habbe, "College Recruitment in 1955," *Management Record*, January, 1955, it is found that a 1950 college graduate entering business in that year was paid on the average a starting salary of $1,775, adjusted. In five years his adjusted income has risen to $3,068, over

TABLE 28
Annual Salaries of Teachers in Rural and Rural-Urban Counties, and in Metropolitan Counties in the South by Race, 1939-40 and 1951-52

[*Adjusted for price changes**]

	1939-40		1951-52		PERCENT INCREASE 1939-40 TO 1951-52	
	White	Negro	White	Negro	White	Negro
Rural................	800	405	1,250	1,150	56.3	184.0
Rural-Urban..........	837	462	1,360	1,219	62.5	163.9
Metropolitan.........	1,321	786	1,663	1,588	25.9	102.0

TABLE 29
Annual Salaries of Teachers in South and Southern States by Race, 1939-40 and 1951-52

[*Adjusted for price changes**]

	1939-40		1951-52		PERCENTAGE INCREASE 1939-40 TO 1951-52	
	White	Negro	White	Negro	White	Negro
South†............	962	505	1,460	1,273	51.8	152.1
Alabama........	850	403	1,359	1,257	59.9	211.9
Arkansas........	627	369	1,028	812	64.0	120.0
Florida..........	1,118	578	1,702	1,557	52.2	169.4
Georgia.........	865	391	1,385	1,284	60.1	228.4
Louisiana........	1,049	391	1,649	1,420	57.1	263.2
Mississippi......	778	233	1,061	543	36.3	133.0
N. Carolina......	990	718	1,523	1,564	53.8	117.8
Oklahoma.......	1,000	973	1,587	1,590	58.7	63.4
S. Carolina......	941	389	1,409	1,058	49.7	172.0
Tennessee.......	860	652	1,141	1,195	32.7	83.3
Texas............	1,122	682	1,707	1,640	52.1	140.5
Virginia.........	971	614	1,338	1,373	37.7	123.6

*Figures shown in 1935-39 dollars.
†Averages for 12 states reporting.

$1,400 more than the average salary of white teachers employed in metropolitan schools and $1,460 more than that of Negro teachers in metropolitan schools.

The shortage of well-qualified teachers is largely explained by these comparisons.

Chapter 5

What the South Is Spending for Schooling

TOTAL SCHOOL COSTS IN THE SOUTH, 1951-52

These rather sizable figures portray the broad features of the South's educational outlays and effort in the base year, 1951-52. They represent the broad categories of expenditures that any school system must meet. First, there are the current expenditures: instruction, a group of miscellaneous expenditures related to book acquisitions, maintenance and operations, and so on. Second, there is transportation. Third, there are capital expenditures: the outlays in plant and equipment. And finally there are the financing costs: interest on debt and payments toward debt retirement.

The thirteen states paid out a total of over $1,631,000,000 to meet these many requirements in 1951-52. Instruction absorbed the biggest share, $889,000,000, or 55 per cent; transportation, in a sense a non-educational expense, 5 per cent; the miscellany, 15 per cent; capital outlay, 19 per cent; and debt service, 6 per cent.

The expenditure called "capital outlay" is for any one year not necessarily representative of the efforts to improve housing for the school children of the South, for these expenditures are intermittent rather than running expenses. Therefore, they vary greatly from year to year. While $315 million is high, it may be less than the outlay in some years and greater than that in others.

On the other hand, instruction is a running expense and, as a rule, tends to remain at about the same relative level year in and year out. But in any one year, given the tremendous variations in capital outlay, instruction may drop as a percentage of total expenditures when outlays for plant and equipment are raised.

In 1951-52 Alabama's and Oklahoma's instruction costs ran 71 and 70 per cent of total costs, respectively. But this was a year in which capital outlays had fallen significantly for both, to 8 per cent for Alabama and to 5 per cent for Oklahoma. As a rule, instruction expenditures tend to run somewhere between 50 and 60 per cent of the total expenditures, given something like 15 to 25 per cent for capital outlays.

To be sure, some states already having made sizable capital outlays in previous years will now be faced with higher charges for debt servicing than those states whose capital expansion programs have been retarded for one reason or the other. Thus Virginia, having just initiated a large building program, is currently expending 36 per cent of its funds on capital needs and, therefore, its instruction

TABLE 30
Public School Expenditures for South and Southern States, 1951-52

	Current Expenditures			
	Instruction	Transportation	Other	Total
South............	$889,141,618	$80,664,198	$249,922,316	$1,219,728,132
Alabama........	60,133,367	5,640,985	9,770,815	75,545,167
Arkansas........	25,978,154	4,152,820	6,994,424	37,125,398
Florida.........	68,879,759	3,788,943	15,910,437	88,579,139
Georgia.........	74,000,828	9,230,177	19,363,035	102,594,040
Kentucky.......	48,316,962	4,955,369	17,347,924	70,620,255
Louisiana.......	58,777,684	7,762,687	29,751,900	96,292,271
Mississippi.....	29,178,809	5,290,008	7,599,274	42,068,091
N. Carolina†....	90,901,261	6,486,084	27,646,674	125,034,019
Oklahoma......	60,983,885‡	4,748,796	16,902,930	82,635,611
S. Carolina.....	44,213,376	1,967,211	12,233,060	58,413,647
Tennessee......	60,207,640	6,248,033	18,667,091	85,122,764
Texas...........	202,077,670	14,951,340	50,993,828	268,022,838
Virginia........	65,492,223	5,441,745	16,740,924	87,674,892

	Capital Outlay	Debt Service	Total Expenditures
South............	$314,905,741	$96,809,606	$1,631,443,479
Alabama..........	7,187,373	2,090,959	84,832,499
Arkansas.........	10,338,240	5,074,001	52,537,639
Florida...........	34,554,771	9,674,500	132,808,410
Georgia...........	14,486,866	8,900,704	125,981,610
Kentucky.........	5,322,710	10,456,108	86,399,073
Louisiana.........	22,418,131	9,598,238	128,308,640
Mississippi.......	14,225,525	n.a.	56,293,616*
N. Carolina†.....	47,218,108	6,834,622	179,086,749
Oklahoma........	4,648,107	160,364‡	87,424,082
S. Carolina.......	8,136,089	2,708,300	69,258,036
Tennessee........	23,067,131	3,100,855	111,290,750
Texas............	71,881,273	33,845,889§	373,750,000§
Virginia..........	51,441,417	4,365,066	143,481,375

n.a.—not available.
*Does not include debt service.
†1950-51 data.
‡Includes salaries of teachers, principals, and superintendents only; instructional materials not included.
‡Includes interest only.
§Estimated.

expenditures have fallen to 45 per cent. Florida, Mississippi, and Tennessee are in somewhat the same position.

Other expenditures tend to vary owing partly to differences in the kinds of auxiliary educational services rendered and partly to the extent of maintenance of plant and equipment.

THE NEGRO'S SHARE OF SCHOOL DOLLARS

The Negro's percentage of the white school dollar as measured by expenditures per pupil has gradually increased since 1931-32. But this slow increase represents the reversal of a long-time trend beginning in the 1870's and continuing until about 1930.

Between 1865 and the end of Congressional Reconstruction in 1877, Southern states made fundamental commitments to public education and the education of Negro children. During this twelve-year period school funds were meager, but the fragmentary evidence available indicates that expenditures were relatively even-handed between the races. As the control of the former Confederate states was returned to the hands of the traditional leaders of the states, all public schools faced retrenchment, and later when school development regained its momentum, the inadequate school funds were more and more directed toward the white children. By the time of the famous dictum implicitly approving the doctrine of "separate but equal" schools for Negroes in the *Plessy* v. *Ferguson* decision by the Supreme Court in 1896, Negro expenditures per child had probably dropped to little more than half of the white expenditures.

In 1900 the expenditure on the Negro child was approximately 50 per cent of the white, according to incomplete records, and this percentage continued to decline despite growth of the public school sentiment in the region. School funds were insufficient however they were used, and they were spent primarily on whites. The Negro expenditure as a percentage of white expenditures continued to decline until about 1930, and then the trend turned slowly upward. For the six Southern states for which relatively continuous expenditures by race have been found for the last two decades, the Negro per-pupil expenditure stood at 29.6 per cent of the white in 1931-32. As the bottom of the depression was passed, the Negro percentage moved slightly upward, 34.6 per cent in 1935-36 and 37.4 per cent in 1937-38. The Negro gains accelerated as World War II brought new levels of income to Southern states, and by 1945-46 the Negro percentage

TABLE 31

Expenditure per Pupil for Current Expenses Less Transportation for Six Southern States by Race, 1931-32 through 1951-52*

	White	Negro	Negro as Percentage of White
1931-32†	39.09	11.56	29.6
1935-36	37.70	13.06	34.6
1937-38‡	44.59	16.70	37.4
1939-40	44.40	18.58	41.8
1941-42	51.67	22.76	44.0
1943-44	68.39	30.76	45.0
1945-46	80.29	44.84	55.8
1947-48	120.21	74.85	61.9
1949-50	130.03	86.88	66.3
1951-52	153.39	112.63	73.4

SOURCE: Calculated from data in reports of state departments of education and from reports of U.S. Office of Education.
*States included are Alabama, Arkansas, Florida, Georgia, North Carolina, South Carolina.
†Includes transportation.
‡Calculated from teacher salaries.

reached 55.8 per cent. The increase continued in succeeding years until Negro expenditures were almost three-fourths of the white in 1951-52.

These percentages are undoubtedly somewhat lower than would be the comparable figures for some of the states omitted here because of data limitations. For example, Kentucky, Tennessee, and Virginia are approaching equalization on a statewide basis, and Oklahoma has fully achieved it.

The six states of Table 31, mostly in the deep South, were within sight of the requirement of the *Plessy* decision, although fifty years late, as one Southern governor said when the Supreme Court handed down its sweeping constitutional decision on May 17, 1954.

TOTAL CURRENT EXPENDITURES FOR
WHITES AND NEGROES

Current expenditures cover the outlays for administration and control, instruction, school operation, lunch programs, and related activities. *Expenditures on transportation, buildings, and equipment are excluded.*

Table 32 gives a comparison of the total current expenditures by races for the Southern states for 1939-40 and 1951-52. All data are stated in 1951-52 dollars to eliminate the effects of changes in the general price level. The data for several states are estimated since no breakdowns by race were available. (See Appendix 2.)

Taking the Southern states together, the total current expenditures on white pupils have risen to $925.3 million in 1951-52, an increase since 1939-40 of $430.8 million, or 87 per cent. The increase in total current expenditures for the Negro pupils is $147.0 million, or just over 200 per cent. This great difference vividly portrays the effort made in the South in the last decade to improve Negro education. While Table 32 takes into account the inflation since 1939-40, it does not reflect the changes in school-age population; this adjustment will be developed in the next table. Setting population changes aside for the moment, therefore, the significance of this table is that, in spite of the great inflation, the South is making prodigious strides toward new goals in education.

This development is evident, of course, in the spending by individual states. Louisiana has increased its spending on Negro pupils by 356 per cent. Georgia and Alabama follow closely, their outlays running 325 and 310 per cent, respectively. Only one Southern state has not doubled its real expenditures on its Negro pupils, Oklahoma; but Oklahoma, as will be seen, had achieved equalization by 1939-40, and the increase of nearly 50 per cent indicates its continuing efforts to improve Negro education.

No state has advanced current expenditures for white pupils to the same degree percentagewise as for Negro pupils. Florida scores the highest white increase, 139 per cent. Only two other states exceed the hundred mark, Georgia and Louisiana, with 122 and 108 per cent increases, respectively. While raising its spending on Negro pupils 167 per cent, Mississippi increased its spending on white pupils only 48 per cent.

TABLE 32

Total Current Expenditures for South and Southern States by Race, 1939-40 and 1951-52

[*Figures given to nearest million of 1951-52 dollars*]

	1939-40		1951-52	
	White	Negro	White	Negro
South............	$494.5	$73.1	$925.3	$220.1
Alabama.........	28.8	5.1	49.0	20.9
Arkansas.........	16.0	2.3	27.3	5.6
Florida..........	28.2	4.5	67.5	17.3
Georgia..........	33.5	5.6	74.4	23.8
Kentucky........	37.8*	1.8*	61.6*	4.1*
Louisiana........	30.5	5.5	63.5	25.1
Mississippi.......	19.4	3.0	28.8	8.0
N. Carolina......	43.9	11.9	87.7	30.9
Oklahoma........	49.7	4.3	73.0*	6.3*
S. Carolina......	21.3	4.7	39.0	17.4
Tennessee........	36.3*	4.5*	66.5*	12.4*
Texas............	116.0*	12.2*	225.1	28.0
Virginia..........	33.1*	7.7*	61.9*	20.3*

*These data are estimated.

EXPENDITURES PER PUPIL

Current expenditures as developed in Table 32 should be related to the school population. The customary and best way to accomplish this is to divide the total current expenditure figures by the number of pupils in average daily attendance. Table 33 presents the data so derived. Because four states do not report breakdowns by race, the expenditures on white and Negro pupils in these states have been estimated. (See Appendix 2.) Again, transportation expenditures, having no direct bearing on the quality of education, are excluded.

The South on the average was spending in 1951-52 approximately $166 per white pupil and $116 per Negro pupil in average daily attendance. For the white pupils this represents an increase of $72, or 76 per cent, since 1939-40; for the Negro pupils, an increase of $75, or 185 per cent. This large increase is obviously consistent with the changes in total current expenditures developed in Table 32.

Despite the spectacular increase in Negro expenditures, the growth in white expenditures continued for the region as a whole at such a rate that the dollar gap between the current expenditures for the two races remained almost unchanged during the period; it was $53.85 in 1939-40 and $50.15 in 1951-52. Hence, only a slight gain in dollar equalization of current expenditures had been achieved.

Of the states, Georgia has made the greatest effort percentagewise to raise the level of expenditures for Negro pupils. Starting from $27.51 per pupil in 1939-40, it boosted its expenditures to $114.44 by 1951-52, an increase of 307 per cent. Alabama and Louisiana come the nearest to this effort. Between 1939-40 and 1951-52, Alabama's expenditure per Negro pupil rose from $26.08 to $102.25, a percentage rise of 292. Louisiana's increased from $38.28 to $148.38, a gain of 280 per cent.

Three states which spent more per Negro pupil in 1939-40 raised the 1951-52 expenditure over the dollar expenditures of the above states. Texas was spending at the rate of $158.13 per Negro pupil in average daily attendance in 1951-52; Florida, $153.24 per Negro pupil; and Oklahoma $195.75.

The white pupils, of course, have fared better in dollar expenditures over the twelve-year period. In 1939-40 Negro pupils fared as well as or better than the white pupils in only one state—again, Oklahoma. In the same year the lowest expenditure per white pupil

TABLE 33

Current Expenditures per Pupil in Average Daily Attendance for South and Southern States by Race, 1939-40 and 1951-52

[*Figures given in 1951-52 dollars*]

	1939-40		1951-52	
	White	Negro	White	Negro
South	$ 94.41	$ 40.56	$165.71	$115.56
Alabama	77.92	26.08	127.72	102.25
Arkansas	56.68	24.50	102.05	67.75
Florida	118.21	51.52	195.01	153.24
Georgia	87.94	27.51	173.10	114.44
Kentucky	78.92*	49.60*	137.84*	130.68*
Louisiana	119.74	38.28	229.08	148.38
Mississippi	78.54	13.63	117.43	35.27
N. Carolina	78.50	51.41	152.20	128.67
Oklahoma	111.29	118.27	195.75*	195.75*
S. Carolina	95.68	28.55	159.34	95.65
Tennessee	81.42*	50.09*	133.75*	126.53*
Texas	123.02*	70.31*	208.60*	158.13*
Virginia	90.06*	61.61*	148.42*	145.30*

*These data are estimated from the data in Table 32.

was found in Arkansas, $77.92; the highest, Texas, with $123.02 per white pupil. In 1951-52 Arkansas had increased the rate by 80 per cent to $102.05 per white pupil; Texas by 70 per cent to $208.50 per pupil. Georgia, again, made the greatest effort percentagewise; the expenditure of $87.94 in 1939-40 rose in 1951-52 to $173.10 per white pupil, an increase of 97 per cent.

CITY AND COUNTRY SCHOOL DOLLARS

Equalization at the local as well as the state level is of course a major part of the school problem of the South. Its evaluation is an insuperable task; however, some understanding of its magnitude can be gained from an examination of current expenditure in sample subdivisions of the states.

Relatively complete data for metropolitan areas and sample data for rural areas are presented in Table 34.

As might be expected, the greatest expenditures have been made in metropolitan school districts. In 1940 for the whole South the metropolitan districts were spending $53.89 per pupil in average daily attendance, while the rural districts were spending only $32.98. Thus the rural expenditures were only 61 per cent of the metropolitan.

As is true of the states as single units, there is considerable variation in spending from state to state by metropolitan districts. The range in 1939-40 was from a low of $34.80 for Mississippi to a high of $83.28 for Kentucky. The range in 1951-52 was from a low of $119.85 for Mississippi to a high of $265.75 for Kentucky.

The same sort of variability is found in the rural districts. The range there was from $20.54 in 1940 for Arkansas to a high of $53.67 for Florida. For 1951-52, the range was from $56.46 for Mississippi to $211.73 for Texas.

Stating rural as a percentage of metropolitan expenditures affords another measure. In 1940, five states—Arkansas, Georgia, Mississippi, Tennessee, and Virginia—were actually spending less than 60 per cent of the metropolitan current expenditures on their rural schools. For the region as a whole, the ratio is 61 per cent. But by 1952 this gap had been partly closed. For the region, the rural-metropolitan ratio had reached 75. On the basis of the data available, the lowest percentage is Kentucky's 44 and the highest, Texas' 104. Admittedly, since the rural data are on a sample basis, there may be enough variation in the samples to account partly for the differences found.

The contrasts in the spending by school districts are all the more pronounced when the expenditures are broken down by race, as in Table 35. Unfortunately, data for only seven states and only on 1951-52 are available, but even these are revealing.

The Negro expenditure as a percentage of white was lowest in Mississippi, 33 per cent in its rural districts; but in its metropolitan areas Mississippi is spending upon Negro pupils 51 per cent of the amount spent on white pupils. North Carolina is the high state with 79 per cent in rural districts and 95 per cent in metropolitan. But these data do not tell the entire story, for there are states not included in this table in which equalization has occurred or is being approached.

TABLE 34
Current Expenditures per Pupil in Metropolitan Districts and Sample Rural Districts, and Rural as Percentage of Metropolitan, 1939-40 and 1951-52

	Metropolitan Districts		Rural Districts		Rural as Percentage of Metropolitan	
	1939-40	1951-52	1939-40	1951-52	1939-40	1951-52
South	$53.89	$178.23	$32.98	$133.40	61	75
Alabama	40.70	131.59	27.11	110.32	67	84
Arkansas	43.80	129.35	20.54	91.80	47	71
Florida	61.13	199.71	53.67	169.86	88	85
Georgia	56.73	169.40	30.23	129.23	53	76
Kentucky	83.28	265.75	n.a.	116.39	..	44
Louisiana	63.14	233.31	44.80	178.79	71	77
Mississippi	34.80	119.85	20.70	56.46	59	47
N. Carolina	44.51	167.34	34.75	130.97	78	78
Oklahoma	n.a.	206.56	n.a.	189.07	..	92
S. Carolina	45.24	150.40	29.92	114.30	66	76
Tennessee	54.68	154.69	32.39	125.74	59	81
Texas	n.a.	204.30	n.a.	211.73	..	104
Virginia	64.80	184.77	35.70	109.54	55	59

n.a.—Not available.

TABLE 35
Current Expenditures per Pupil in Metropolitan Districts and Sample Rural Districts by Race, 1951-52

	Metropolitan Districts		Rural Districts		Negro as Percentage of White	
	White	Negro	White	Negro	Met.	Rural
Seven States	$166.32	$126.45	$138.24	$ 85.10	76	62
Alabama	147.20	105.40	122.14	96.41	72	79
Arkansas	135.74	111.58	97.71	67.24	82	69
Florida	204.58	179.54	189.51	119.22	88	63
Georgia	184.57	132.66	147.34	89.79	72	61
Mississippi	152.30	78.11	82.73	27.05	51	33
N. Carolina	169.64	161.14	148.98	117.23	95	79
S. Carolina	170.21	116.75	179.31	78.77	69	44

INSTRUCTION COSTS AS A PERCENTAGE OF CURRENT EXPENDITURES

While the degree to which an educational program is being bettered cannot be wholly quantitatively measured, the patterns of enrichment can be traced by the behavior of instruction expenditures over a period of time. Generally speaking, the smaller the proportion of current expenditures consumed by instruction, the greater the outlay for enrichment programs. This is true, however, only when salaries and current expenditures for maintenance and operating costs remain relatively constant. On this basis, the development of enrichment programs for white and Negro pupils may be roughly inferred from Tables 36 and 37.

Table 36 states instruction as a percentage of total current expense in six Southern states. Data for this group point up what is, with few exceptions, a fairly general condition in the South: instruction costs are a large percentage of current expenditures, and the percentages for the Negro are greater than those for the white pupils. This difference gives some evidence of the tendency for these states to make relatively low outlays on enrichment programs for both races, and particularly for Negro pupils.

However, there is a trend toward lower ratios for both races, evidence of a general attempt to enrich educational services.

Although there are differences in these efforts between states, no conclusive evaluation can be made of them because of the fact that there are significant internal changes in total current expenditures.

Table 37 demonstrates that the instruction expenditures per white pupil in ADA in relation to the instruction expenditures per Negro pupil in ADA are changing in two directions. First, more and more funds for instructional purposes are being allocated to the Negro pupils compared to the allocation to the white pupils by the geographical breakdowns, rural, rural-urban, and metropolitan school districts. Thus, in rural schools the ratio of white to Negro pupil expenditures on instruction in high Negro population areas was 4:1 in 1939-40; by 1951-52, the spread between the two races in similar areas had decreased significantly as is indicated by the ratio of 1.59:1. In metropolitan school districts with high Negro population, the ratio was 2.79:1 in 1939-40; in 1951-52, it had dropped to 1.13:1, or near equalization of expenditures on instruction.

Second, the table shows that instructional expenditures on Negro pupils in districts of high Negro population are approaching the level of expenditures on white pupils in areas of high Negro popula-

TABLE 36

Instruction as a Percentage of Current Expense in Public Schools of Six Southern States by Race, 1939-40 and 1951-52

	1939-40		1951-52	
	White	Negro	White	Negro
Alabama	75.2	87.2	77.0	85.7
Arkansas	71.6	75.7	69.8	70.6
Florida	76.0	82.6	76.4	83.0
Georgia	75.6	85.3	68.9	82.0
N. Carolina	75.9	83.3	70.6	78.5
S. Carolina	76.4	84.1	73.5	80.4

TABLE 37

Median Ratios of Instruction Expenditures per White Pupil to Instruction Expenditures per Negro Pupil in Average Daily Attendance in Sample Rural and Rural-Urban, and in Metropolitan Counties with High and Low Percentages of Negro Population in Nine Southern States, 1939-40, 1949-50, and 1951-52

County Classification	1939-40		1949-50		1951-52	
	High County	Low County	High County	Low County	High County	Low County
Rural	4.00:1	2.15:1	1.74:1	1.23:1	1.59:1	1.19:1
Rural-Urban	3.55:1	1.77:1	1.63:1	1.20:1	1.46:1	1.02:1
Metropolitan	2.79:1	1.96:1	1.39:1	1.22:1	1.13:1	0.94:1

tion. Thus, in metropolitan areas of low Negro population the instructional expenditures on white pupils in relation to Negroes were 1.96:1 in 1939-40. By 1951-52, the ratio had moved in the other direction, 0.94:1; so that relatively more is being spent on Negro than on white pupils.

THE INFLUENCE OF INCOME AND PLACE OF RESIDENCE ON EXPENDITURES PER PUPIL

In Table 38 the expenditures for instruction per white child and per Negro child in average daily attendance for the years 1939-40, 1949-50, and 1951-52 are shown according to the kind of county in which the pupil lived—rural, rural-urban, and metropolitan. The county classifications are further subdivided into high-income and low-income counties. This table is not based upon all of the thirteen hundred counties of the region but upon a directed sample of approximately one hundred counties.

In 1939-40 children in metropolitan counties received higher expenditures per pupil than children of the same race in rural-urban and rural counties. All the high-income counties spent more per pupil than did the low-income counties of the same type.

In 1949-50 the high-income counties again spent more than the low-income counties in the same category, but the rural and rural-urban children in high-income counties were equal to the low-income metropolitan counties. In 1951-52 the pattern was more consistent; the high-income counties spent more than the low-income counties in each classification, and metropolitan counties, high and low, spent more than rural-urban, but the high-income rural counties spent more than low-income rural-urban counties.

In sum, this table demonstrates that expenditures for current expenses are heavily influenced by the place of residence in which the child lives, whether rural, rural-urban, or metropolitan, and further that the counties of whatever type where incomes are high are those most likely to be making adequate expenditures for public schools.

It is notable that from 1939-40 to 1951-52 the Negro child received an increasingly more equitable share of the school dollar. In these various classifications of counties the range of the percentage of the Negro expenditure was from 33 to 46 per cent in 1939-40, but by 1951-52 it had been stepped upward to a range of 62 to 87 per cent.

TABLE 38

Expenditure per Pupil in Average Daily Attendance for Instruction in High and Low Income Sample Rural-Urban and Rural Counties and Metropolitan Counties by Race, 1939-40, 1949-50, and 1951-52

	1939-40		1949-50		1951-52	
	White	Negro	White	Negro	White	Negro
High Metropolitan.....	$56.38	$25.87	$136.82	$102.23	$153.44	$111.21
High Rural-Urban.....	42.69	16.09	108.06	72.89	122.87	96.30
High Rural...........	39.63	12.94	109.30	73.40	118.50	84.93
Low Metropolitan.....	45.42	17.30	106.12	69.54	124.09	107.31
Low Rural-Urban.....	32.75	11.82	95.99	60.12	110.41	72.67
Low Rural............	33.22	11.13	91.55	53.24	104.04	68.67

CAPITAL EXPENDITURE PER PUPIL

Capital outlay is the expenditure on school plant and equipment. Stated as dollars spent per pupil in ADA, it varies much more from state to state, and from year to year in a given state, than do current expenditures, for the reason that capital outlays are postponable.

Notwithstanding the year-to-year variations, it may be seen in Table 39 there is a definite upward trend in capital outlay state by state in the South. For the region there has been an increase of 667 per cent from 1939-40 to 1951-52. To be sure, a portion of this increase may be attributed to rising construction and equipment costs. But a sizable amount reflects the efforts of the South to cope with accumulated deficiencies in plant and equipment and with the rising enrollment.

Florida has increased its capital outlays per pupil from $4.90 to $75.29, or 1437 per cent; its expenditures for this purpose had nearly reached the national level of $45.00 per pupil for the fiscal year 1949-50. Texas' outlay of $43.96 in 1949-50 is close to the national figure, while Louisiana's $49.62 and Tennessee's $46.05 exceed it. By 1951-52 all states were making notable progress, increases of over 1400 per cent being recorded by Georgia as well as Florida. Mississippi, starting from a low of $2.35 per pupil in 1939-40, reached $30.17 per pupil in 1951-52, an increase of 1184 per cent.

TABLE 39

Expenditure per Pupil in Average Daily Attendance for Capital Outlay in the Public Schools of South and Southern States, 1939-40, 1949-50, and 1951-52, and Percentage Increase, 1939-40 to 1951-52

	1939-40	1949-50	1951-52	Percentage Increase 1939-40 to 1951-52
South	$ 5.49	$30.12	$42.09	667
Alabama	4.58	14.36	12.24	167
Arkansas	2.60	38.35	29.47	1034
Florida	4.90	42.50	75.29	1437
Georgia	1.48	17.11	22.72	1435
Kentucky	3.55	10.64	11.14	214
Louisiana	14.63	49.62	50.30	244
Mississippi	2.35	6.20	29.83	1184
N. Carolina	4.82	35.10	57.86	1100
Oklahoma	1.67	11.51	11.43	584
S. Carolina	3.89	17.58	19.04	390
Tennessee	8.02	46.05	38.80	384
Texas	7.19	43.96	57.25	696
Virginia	10.86	39.77	92.39	751

CURRENT EXPENDITURES, SOUTH AND NATION

A comparison of the rates of current expenditures in the South with those in the nation should point up the magnitude of educational deficits and the efforts being made to overcome them. Consider the decade between the fiscal years 1939-40 and 1949-50. During this period the rise in current expenditures in the South relative to the nation as a whole has been phenomenal. Table 40 makes this comparison through actual and "deflated" data (in this case, adjusted to state all expenditures in terms of 1935-39 dollars). From the deflated data it is seen that the South enlarged its expenditures per pupil in ADA over the decade by $36.51, or over 78 per cent. The nation as a whole increased its spending per pupil by $33.57, or barely 38 per cent.

There is a somewhat more precise and revealing method of comparing efforts, the use of annual rates of increase over the decade. These may be determined by applying the compound interest formula. Using this method the annual rate of increase for the continental United States is 3.29 per cent during this period; for the South, 5.94 per cent. (See Appendix 3.)

In any case, the relative effort in the South to improve administration, instruction, and operation may thus be said to be nearly twice as great as that of the nation.

TABLE 40

Current Expenditures per Pupil in Average Daily Attendance in South and United States, Actual and Deflated, 1939-40 and 1949-50

[Deflated figures stated in 1935-39 dollars]

	1939-40		1949-50	
	Actual	Deflated	Actual	Deflated
South.............	$46.84	$46.75	$143.13	$ 83.26
United States........	88.09	87.91	208.83	121.48

Part Two

Public Education in the South Tomorrow

Chapter 6

Projection of School-Age Population, Enrollment, and Average Daily Attendance

THE 1960 SCHOOL-AGE POPULATION

The projection of school-age population is for four age groups: 5-6, 7-13, 14-15, and 16-17. The sum of the first two represents the expected elementary-grade population and includes the expected rise in that portion of the population which would enter kindergarten. The sum of the second two groups should approximate the secondary school population.

The total school-age population, 5-17 inclusive, is expected to increase to 13,500,000 by 1960. This increase of 3,570,000 over the 1950 figure reflects largely the upping of the birth rate in the 1940's and the early 1950's. No adjustment for migration is made, on the assumption that by 1960 the out- and in-migration may come close to washing out the difference of the 1940's decade. As the South advances industrially, out-migration should decrease as in-migration rises. Even if out-migration at the 1940's rate continues, however, it may not be very consequential from the standpoint of the fundamental issues involved, since the greatest migration has usually occurred among persons 18 and older.

The total expected white school-age population of 9,837,000 represents an increase of 2,479,000 over 1950, and the Negro population of 3,639,000, an increase of 1,067,000. The projected Negro growth is thus relatively the greater of the two. This expectation is based partly on an anticipated decline in the rate of out-migration of the Negro and partly on an anticipated natural rise in Negro population; the natural rise will reflect improvement in the general well-being and health of the race, a consequence in turn of the growth of Southern productivity and real income.

Percentagewise, the increases in total school-age population will vary considerably from state to state: Alabama, 26.4; Arkansas, 21.4; Florida, 51.4; Georgia, 37.1; Kentucky, 28; Louisiana, 40.6; Mississippi, 31.3; North Carolina, 31.8; Oklahoma, 22.6; South Carolina, 34.5; Tennessee, 29.5; Texas, 50.3; and Virginia, 37.5. Obviously, Florida, Texas, and Louisiana will be confronted with the largest increases for which to provide added educational facilities and in-

TABLE 41

1960 School-Age Population, Ages 5-6, 7-13, 14-15, 16-17, and Total for South and Southern States by Race

[*Figures given to nearest 1,000 persons*]

	WHITE					NEGRO					Total School-Age Population
	5-6	7-13	14-15	16-17	Total	5-6	7-13	14-15	16-17	Total	
South.........	1,729	5,556	1,260	1,292	9,837	655	2,096	453	435	3,639	13,476
Alabama....	101	343	84	89	617	66	224	49	46	385	1,002
Arkansas....	62	242	60	63	427	28	93	21	20	162	589
Florida.....	119	337	75	76	607	42	127	25	23	217	824
Georgia.....	133	416	94	96	739	76	240	52	50	418	1,157
Kentucky...	139	492	110	114	855	11	34	7	7	59	914
Louisiana...	94	318	71	72	555	64	204	42	41	351	906
Mississippi..	55	195	45	48	343	74	238	52	50	414	757
N. Carolina.	161	516	120	123	920	78	249	56	52	435	1,355
Oklahoma...	86	313	75	78	552	13	41	9	9	72	624
S. Carolina..	76	234	53	55	418	63	201	46	45	355	773
Tennessee...	135	468	108	112	823	32	104	21	21	178	1,001
Texas......	434	1,247	266	265	2,212	64	199	40	40	343	2,555
Virginia....	134	435	99	101	769	44	142	33	31	250	1,019

struction, while Arkansas, Kentucky, Oklahoma, and Tennessee will have less difficulty.

No data have been included to show the year-by-year growth for either the states or the region. A simple but fairly accurate annual figure could be obtained by taking the increases in school-age population from 1950 to 1960 and dividing it by ten.

In short, the South is faced with the greatest problem in public education in its history. By 1960 it must provide housing and instruction for over 3,000,000 more pupils; put otherwise, 100,000 or more classrooms and teachers must be added to the present number if the increment in ages 5-17 of the school-age population is to receive an education at least comparable to that now available.

THE ESTIMATION OF SCHOOL ENROLLMENT RATIOS TO 1960

Estimated school enrollment is derived from estimates of school-age population. The population figures are multiplied by appropriate enrollment percentages for the required age groups; the resulting product is the estimated school enrollment. (The technical features of this process are developed in Appendix 4.)

The present percentages of enrollment of school-age children in the public schools of the South are: 34 per cent in the age group 5-6; 91 per cent in the age group 7-13; 85 per cent in the age group 14-15; and 63 per cent in the age group 16-17, inclusive. These ratios or percentages reflect the fact that a portion of the children attend private and parochial schools.

These actual ratios are not applied in the projection of enrollment, since they do not include an allowance for increase in enrollment. Inasmuch as the educational program is being improved and expanded, it may very well be argued that the enrollment ratio will be higher in the future. It will probably move towards the experience of those Southern states which have most notably improved their schools and instruction and, particularly, such states as Oklahoma, Florida, and Georgia, where general equalization is close to achievement or is an accomplished fact. On the basis of the experience of these states, it may be predicted that by 1960 all of the Southern states will attain across-the-board equalization and a significant general improvement of schools and instruction. The future enrollment ratio is thus expected to equal Oklahoma's present ratio and may be even greater.

With this proposition in mind, projected enrollment figures for 1960 may be fully developed as shown in Table 42. These ratios reflect for each of the four age groups the experience of Oklahoma and the other high enrollment states in the South. Several adjustments are made. The last two age groups are increased beyond the experience of the high enrollment states, in order to give effect to expectations about future school attendance. The overall and the state ratios are also modified to reflect the ratio of public school enrollment to total school enrollment in each state. Those states with a relatively high private and parochial enrollment naturally have smaller ratios than do the others.

The projected ratios thus derived for the four age groups for the South as a whole are 38, 97, 94, 79. The overall percentages obtained for the South on this propected basis exceed the national percentages, which are 33, 84, 81, and 68 for the four age groups.

TABLE 42

Basic and Adjusted Enrollment Ratios for South and Southern States to Be Applied in Enrollment Projection

	Age Group			
	5-6	7-13	14-15	16-17
Basic.............	38	97	94	79
South.............	36	93	90	76
Alabama.........	37	94	91	77
Arkansas.........	37	95	92	77
Florida..........	36	92	90	75
Georgia..........	37	96	93	78
Kentucky........	34	87	85	71
Louisiana........	32	81	79	66
Mississippi.......	37	94	91	77
N. Carolina......	38	96	93	78
Oklahoma........	37	94	92	77
S. Carolina......	38	96	93	78
Tennessee........	37	94	92	77
Texas............	36	91	89	74
Virginia..........	37	94	91	76

PROJECTED 1960 ENROLLMENT

To derive the enrollment in 1960, the target year of this study, the estimated school-age populations for each of the four age groups, 5-6, 7-13, 14-15, and 16-17, are multiplied by the projected enrollment ratios or percentages for each age group, shown in Table 42. This process is carried out for each state.

The total enrollment of 10,748,000 in 1960 for the region represents a notable increase over the actual enrollment of around 8,278,000 in the census year 1950, some 2,470,000 more pupils or 29.5 per cent.

Two states will have school enrollments of over a million, North Carolina and Texas—Texas will have nearly two million. The expected enrollment increases over 1950, state by state, vary markedly. The range is from 491,000 for Arkansas to 1,993,000 for Texas. (Arkansas is expected to have the lowest total population growth in the South over the decade.) The percentage change for the states are: Alabama, 20.6; Arkansas, 15.5; Florida, 44.4; Georgia, 33.3; Kentucky, 22.9; Louisiana, 31.9; Mississippi, 15.9; North Carolina, 21.4; Oklahoma, 16.3; South Carolina, 29.8; Tennessee, 24.4; Texas, 50.1; and Virginia, 36.9. The range is thus from 15.5 per cent for Arkansas to 50.1 per cent for Texas.

By age groups, the overall increase is relatively the greatest for the years 16-17. This change reflects the assumption, already discussed, that as schools and instruction are improved the pupils will be induced to remain in school beyond the year of enforced attendance.

TABLE 43

Projected 1960 Enrollment for South and Southern States According to the Projected Ratios

[*Figures given to nearest 1,000 pupils*]

	Age Group				Total
	5-6	7-13	14-15	16-17	
South.............	825	7,076	1,542	1,305	10,748
Alabama.........	62	533	121	104	820
Arkansas........	33	319	75	64	491
Florida..........	58	427	90	75	650
Georgia..........	77	630	136	114	957
Kentucky........	51	457	99	86	693
Louisiana........	51	422	89	75	637
Mississippi.......	48	407	88	76	619
N. Carolina......	49	735	164	137	1,085
Oklahoma........	36	332	78	67	513
S. Carolina.......	53	418	92	78	641
Tennessee........	62	538	118	103	821
Texas............	179	1,316	272	226	1,993
Virginia.........	66	542	120	100	828

RATIO OF AVERAGE DAILY ATTENDANCE TO ENROLLMENT

Looking back at the history of education in the United States over the last forty years, one is struck by the rising demand for schooling. Not only has enrollment as a percentage of total school-age population increased, but average daily attendance as a percentage of enrollment also advanced notably. Forty years ago the percentage had risen to 72; by 1950 it was 88.7, a 17 point increase.

Since growth in attendance is the established pattern, the attendance ratio should be expected to reach an even higher figure by 1960. A study of those states having reached a high level of education for both races supports this assumption. To be sure, there cannot be perfect attendance because of illness and emergencies, but 91 seems reasonable. Interestingly enough, a trend line fitted by mathematical means to the entire range of ratios, 1909 to 1950, yields a projected value when extended to 1960 of 90.8. This projection is essentially identical with the figure 91, derived largely by inference from the experience of states with advanced educational programs. Hence, this projected ratio may not be far from the "true" ratio.

This ratio of 91 will be applied to all the enrollment data for the South and the Southern states to derive the average daily attendance for 1960, the target year.

TABLE 44

Ratio (Percentage) of Average Daily Attendance to Enrollment for Selected Years, 1909-1950, United States

	Percentage Average Daily Attendance to Enrollment
1909-10	72.0
1919-20	74.8
1929-30	82.8
1931-32	84.7
1935-36	84.6
1939-40	86.7
1945-46	85.2
1946-47	86.4
1947-48	87.3
1948-49	87.8
1949-50	88.7

SOURCE: U.S. Office of Education, *Statistics of State School Systems, 1949-50*, p. 15.

AVERAGE DAILY ATTENDANCE FOR 1960

The average daily attendance for 1959-60 is derived simply by multiplying the enrollment expected in 1959-60 by the projected percentage of average daily attendance to enrollment, 91. The computation is made for the region and each state in the South.

Table 45 shows the average daily attendance for the base year, 1951-52, and the target year, 1959-60. The increase for the region is from 7,488,000 to 9,781,000, or 2,293,000. The change amounts to 30.6 per cent. To go back to the census year, 1950, however, for a comparison with the rise in enrollment over the decade, the expected increase in attendance over 1950 is 2,537,000 or 35 per cent as compared with 29.5 per cent for enrollment. This sizable percentage for average daily attendance reflects the compounding into the attendance estimate of the growth in both enrollment and attendance. The percentage increases for the thirteen states are: Alabama, 27.0; Arkansas, 27.4; Florida, 29.0; Georgia, 36.5; Kentucky, 32.0; Louisiana, 30.0; Mississippi, 19.5; North Carolina, 21.0; Oklahoma, 15.3; South Carolina, 36.5; Tennessee, 25.5; Texas, 44.4; and Virginia, 34.9. The average increase for the South is 29.2 per cent. Florida's growth will thus be the regional average. Six states have percentages which lie below this average and six have percentages above it. The distribution is skewed somewhat in the direction of the high ratios.

It may be inferred from this skewness that the largest increase in attendance will take place mainly in those states which are experiencing relatively the greatest ratio of industrial development. To be sure, one or two exceptions may be noted but the generalization appears otherwise to hold. Texas, Georgia, South Carolina, Virginia, and Kentucky have in recent times recorded fairly rapid advances in income attributable considerably to industrialization at a high rate relative to previous decades.

TABLE 45

Average Daily Attendance for 1951-52 and the Projected Average Daily Attendance for 1959-60 for South and Southern States

[*Figures given to nearest 1,000 pupils*]

	1951-52 Average Daily Attendance	1959-60 Average Daily Attendance	Increase of 1959-60 Over 1951-52
South	7,488	9,781	2,293
Alabama	588	746	159
Arkansas	351	447	96
Florida	459	592	133
Georgia	638	871	233
Kentucky	478	631	153
Louisiana	446	580	134
Mississippi	472	563	92
N. Carolina	816	987	171
Oklahoma	405	467	62
S. Carolina	427	583	156
Tennessee	595	747	152
Texas	1,256	1,814	558
Virginia	558	753	195

Chapter 7

The Price of Equality and Improvement

ACROSS-THE-BOARD EQUALIZATION OF CURRENT EXPENDITURES

Whatever the implications of the Supreme Court decision of May 17, 1954, equalization of expenditures for public education between the races will of necessity continue to receive great attention in the South. Moreover, education of both races must be improved to keep pace with the needs of the advancing Southern economy. Equalization for both white and Negro pupils who fall below the target figure represents, in fact, a substantial improvement in the South's public education system.

Given the expected incomes of the several states, the best goal seems to be that which can be sighted by a reasonable number of those states whose expenditures are now low. As already explained, the criterion of $166 per pupil in average daily attendance has been chosen. It is the average current expenditure per white pupil in average daily attendance for the thirteen states in 1951-52, rounded off to the nearest dollar.

To reiterate a definition given earlier, current expenditures cover the outlays for instruction, administration, school, operation, luncheon programs, and related activities. Expenditures on transportation and capital are as before excluded; and so are interest payments, since they are a financial expense not properly allocable to expenses related fairly directly to the educational programs.

"Across-the-board" equalization means bringing current expenditures for both races in the base year, 1951-52, up to the $166 level where not attained and, in those states where the average expenditure is over $166, "across-the-board" equalization means bringing the average expenditure on Negro pupils up to the average of the white pupils. Thus, equalization within and between both races is the goal, state by state, and, implicitly, district by district.

The costs of equalization across the board for the region and each state are developed in Table 46. The total for the region for the base year is $210,000,000. This amount is sufficient to bring the current spending on all students in all states, irrespective of race, up to at least $166 per pupil in average daily attendance and to bring

TABLE 46

Across-the-Board Equalization for South and Southern States, 1951-52

[*Figures given to nearest $1,000*]

	Cost to Equalize		
	White	Negro	Total
South....................	$89,450	120,140	$209,590
Alabama...............	14,590	13,060	27,650
Arkansas..............	17,150	8,130	25,280
Florida................	......	4,750	4,750
Georgia................	......	12,270	12,270
Kentucky..............	12,520	1,090	13,610
Louisiana..............	......	13,690	13,690
Mississippi............	12,000	29,740	41,740
N. Carolina...........	8,060	8,880	16,940
Oklahoma.............	......	None	......
S. Carolina............	1,720	12,740	14,460
Tennessee.............	15,900	3,820	19,720
Texas.................	......	9,030	9,030
Virginia...............	7,510	2,940	10,450

the expenditures upon Negro pupils in the states which are spending more than $166 on white pupils to the level of the white pupils. Thus, in Florida, the current expenditure per white child in average daily attendance is $195.01 and the expenditure upon the Negro child is $153.74. The difference of $41.27 will be made up for each Negro pupil.

The cost is relatively small for some states. Florida's $4,750,000 is the lowest and represents an increase of only 5.6 per cent over the actual 1951-52 current expenditures. The highest outlay would be made by Mississippi, $41,740,000, an increase of around 114 per cent over the 1951-52 actual expenditures. The mean deficiency for the region is around $16,000,000 per state. Oklahoma has already equalized at a goal well above $166 so that it would need make no additional outlay according to this criterion.

ESTIMATED CAPITAL DEFICIT AS OF 1952

A major part of the South's educational program is the elimination of the capital deficit. Children are in many instances housed in buildings far below any conceivable standard of proper housing. The capital deficit is the amount needed to bring the existing plant and equipment up to a minimum standard and to provide adequate space for the existing school population.

Different minimum standards of space per pupil have been adopted in this study for elementary and secondary schools. All buildings for either replacement or expansion purposes will be modern, fireproof, well-ventilated, and well-lighted, designed to provide 45 square feet per pupil at the elementary level and 60 square feet at the secondary level. (Some cities are constructing buildings with significantly more space per pupil but at great costs.)

First, the total space required to house the entire number of students currently in attendance is computed. This total is the product of the standard square feet of space and the number in average daily attendance. It is multiplied in turn by a standard cost per square foot; in Kentucky, North Carolina, Tennessee, and Virginia this cost for the base year is $10.31; in Alabama, Florida, Georgia, Mississippi, and South Carolina, $7.50; and in Arkansas, Louisiana, Oklahoma, and Texas, $10.54.[1] To the total cost so derived must be added an amount to cover equipment needs. Actually total building costs are multiplied by 1.0938, the product of which is total space and equipment needs in base-year dollars. The factor 1.0938 is derived by relating equipment costs to building costs for existing buildings and adding 1.000. The first column in Table 47 contains these costs.

From the total of building and equipment needs a "write-off" deduction is made. This write-off, shown in column 2, is the value of the existing buildings considered adequate and which therefore need not be replaced. The net amount after this subtraction is the capital deficit, the total of building and equipment replacement and expansion needs. (See Appendix 5 for further discussion of methods and computation.)

The total deficit for the South amounts to $1,928,000,000. The absolute deficit per state obviously varies greatly, but fails to reflect the relative status of the state. When the deficit is computed

1. The editors are indebted to Dr. N. E. Viles for counsel on these figures.

TABLE 47

Estimated Capital Deficits for South and Southern States in 1951-52

[*Figures given to nearest million of 1951-52 dollars*]

	Total Cost of Buildings and Equipment Before "Write-off"	Amount of "Write-off"	Current Capital Deficit
South	3,729	1,801	1,928
Alabama	243	47	196
Arkansas	195	54	141
Florida	190	125	65
Georgia	254	130	124
Kentucky	262	76	186
Louisiana	246	142	104
Mississippi	184	61	123
N. Carolina	442	201	241
Oklahoma	227	127	100
S. Carolina	171	73	98
Tennessee	322	98	225
Texas	696	519	177
Virginia	297	149	148

on a per pupil (in ADA) basis, the variability changes pattern. Of the seemingly high states, Texas has a per-pupil deficit of $179; Mississippi, $261 a pupil; and Florida, $142 a pupil.

Needless to say, the total deficit is sizable. A portion of it represents the substandard conditions of Negro schools. By crude estimation, the great gap between expenditures on Negro and white school children for housing accounts roughly for over a third of the above amount, or $800,000,000.

Thus an expenditure of upwards of two billion dollars in plant and equipment equitably allocated between the two races would eliminate the gap in capital outlays on Negro schools and achieve equalization of plant and equipment for the two races. Moreover, it would eliminate substandard buildings now being occupied by both races.

THE ANNUAL GROWTH IN CURRENT AND TRANSPORTATION EXPENDITURES FROM 1952 TO 1960

Once having equalized the expenditures across the board and having provided reasonably adequate housing and equipment for the pupil population existing as of 1952, it remains to meet the anticipated growth in the school-age population from 1952 to 1960.

The first step involves meeting the costs of the growth in current and transportation needs. These needs vary directly with average daily attendance. The increase in attendance, for the sake of simplicity, is assumed to be by even yearly amounts. These annual increments, found in the first column in Table 48, are multiplied by either $166, the average expenditure per white pupil in ADA in the South for 1951-52, or the actual state expenditure per white pupil in ADA, whichever is the larger. For example, Alabama's increment of 15,000 multiplied by $166 gives the anual increment in current expenditure, $2,507,000. For Florida, however, the expenditure per white pupil in ADA is $195; multiply the ADA increment of 17,700 by $195 and the expenditure increment of $3,452,000 is derived. And so on for each state, dependent upon which expenditure value is the greater, the average $166, or the actual.

In Table 48 the usual state-by-state variations appear. Texas has the greatest annual increment and Mississippi the smallest. Texas is spending in 1951-52 $209 per white child in ADA; its expected growth in ADA is the largest, hence its large current expenditure increment.

To the yearly increment in current expenditure is added a provision for transportation costs. As explained above, transportation costs are treated separately from current expenditures. On the assumption that transportation needs will grow proportionately with ADA, a yearly increment in transportation expenditure is derived.

Taken together current and transportation expenditures are expected to grow each year by the amounts entered in Table 48.

Among the factors affecting population and hence enrollment and ADA is migration in and out of a region, state, or county. No adjustment to reflect such changes state by state has been made; the estimates would be too hazardous where so detailed a breakdown is attempted.

TABLE 48

Annual Increments in Average Daily Attendance, Current and Transportation Expenditures for South and Southern States

[Figures given to nearest 1,000 pupils or $1,000]

	Annual Increment in Average Daily Attendance	Annual Increment Current Expenditures	Annual Increment Transportation Expenditures	Total of Increments
South.............	253.7	$46,847	$3,121	$49,968
Alabama.........	15.1	2,507	190	2,697
Arkansas.........	9.2	1,527	140	1,667
Florida..........	17.7	3,452	137	3,589
Georgia..........	25.1	4,342	415	4,757
Kentucky........	15.1	2,507	198	2,705
Louisiana........	15.9	3,641	299	3,940
Mississippi.......	9.1	1,511	132	1,643
N. Carolina......	18.9	3,137	170	3,307
Oklahoma.......	6.5	1,274	89	1,363
S. Carolina......	16.9	2,805	88	2,893
Tennessee.......	16.4	2,722	203	2,925
Texas...........	66.2	13,836	822	14,658
Virginia.........	21.6	3,586	238	3,824

PROVIDING BUILDINGS AND EQUIPMENT FOR SCHOOL POPULATION GROWTH TO 1960

In projecting the capital needs—plant and equipment—to meet the growth in school-age population, the expected enrollment is made the base for projection. Space requirements for a growing population should be planned according to the expected enrollment and not, as was done in estimating the current capital deficit above, according to average daily attendance. To use attendance as the base may lead to serious underestimation of the required space and equipment.

The details of the method of projection are developed in Appendix 6. Only the bare essentials and conclusions are treated here. Three assumptions are involved: (1) that 45 square feet will be provided for each elementary pupil, ages 5-13, and 60 square feet for each secondary pupil, ages 14-17; (2) that 10 per cent of the building cost will cover the school equipment needs; and (3) although costs tend to vary somewhat from section to section in the South, they are assumed to be the same within each state whether the school is in a rural or metropolitan area.

Table 49 shows the total cost of school plant and equipment necessary to meet the growth in enrollment, 1952-1960, and the yearly outlays over this eight-year period, given the above assumptions. The data are stated in 1952 dollars. The annual outlay is simply one-eighth of the total cost, made on the assumption that the growth in enrollment will be relatively even from year to year. This assumption is sufficiently valid, and it definitely simplifies planning for growth.

The total outlay to be made in the South to meet the growth in enrollment over the period is $1,295,113,600; this amount can be met by eight annual appropriations of $161,889,000.

As has been seen, enrollment expectations vary significantly from state to state; thus the capital costs also show large variations. In addition, some variations are attributable to cost differences.

Arkansas' and Oklahoma's 1959-1960 enrollments are the lowest in the South, and their total costs of $64,380,800 and $43,439,000 are also the lowest. North Carolina and Texas, with very sizable increases in enrollment ahead, are faced with corresponding increases in capital costs, $123,280,800 and $332,577,600, respectively.

Implicit in the figures set forth in Table 49 is, of course, the cost of equalization of capital needs for the two races. Both will have equal and improved plant and equipment, relative to their respective enrollments. This great increase in capital outlays obtains whether or not the schools are integrated. There is no evidence that integration in the large would materially change school costs. (See discussion in Appendix 7.)

In Table 50, annual costs to meet the yearly increments in school population for current expenditures, transportation, and schools and equipment are summarized for the region and the individual states.

TABLE 49
Total Costs for School Plant and Equipment for South and Southern States, 1952-1960, and Annual Outlay Over Eight Year Period

	Total Cost 1952-1960 to Meet Growth	Annual Outlay
South	$1,295,113,600	$161,889,200
Alabama	64,380,800	8,047,600
Arkansas	50,218,400	6,277,300
Florida	70,878,400	8,859,800
Georgia	95,095,200	11,886,900
Kentucky	91,884,800	11,485,600
Louisiana	89,508,000	11,188,500
Mississippi	56,112,000	7,014,000
N. Carolina	123,280,800	15,410,100
Oklahoma	43,439,200	5,429,900
S. Carolina	63,790,400	7,973,800
Tennessee	96,892,000	12,111,500
Texas	332,577,600	41,572,200
Virginia	117,056,000	14,632,000

TABLE 50
Total Annual Costs of Equalized Current Expenditures, Transportation, and Equalized Schools and Equipment to Meet the Growth in Average Daily Attendance and Enrollment for South and Southern States

[*Figures given to nearest $1,000*]

	Annual Increment Current Expenditures	Annual Increment Transportation Expenditures	Annual Increment Capital Outlays	Total of Increments
South	$46,847	$3,121	$161,891	$211,859
Alabama	2,507	190	8,048	10,745
Arkansas	1,527	140	6,277	7,944
Florida	3,452	137	8,860	12,449
Georgia	4,342	415	11,887	16,644
Kentucky	2,507	198	11,486	14,191
Louisiana	3,641	299	11,189	15,129
Mississippi	1,511	132	7,014	8,657
N. Carolina	3,137	170	15,410	18,717
Oklahoma	1,274	89	5,430	6,793
S. Carolina	2,805	88	7,974	10,867
Tennessee	2,722	103	12,112	15,037
Texas	13,836	822	41,572	56,230
Virginia	3,586	238	14,632	18,456

Chapter 8

The Projection of Southern Income

THE GROWTH OF SOUTHERN INCOME

The capacity to pay for educational requirements is measurable only in terms of income, and income must grow with increases in expenditures. Income may be shown in total income payments for a state or region or in per capita income. Changes in per capita income are somewhat more descriptive of economic well-being and consequently of the ability to pay. The South's per capita income in current dollars is compared with the non-South's from 1929 to 1952 in Table 51. During this period the Southern per capita income increased from slightly less than half of the non-South figure to approximately two-thirds.

When the data are corrected for price level changes, the South's per capita income is seen as having grown from $304 in 1929 to $632 in 1952, the non-South's from $650 to $954. Thus the South's has doubled, while the non-South's has increased by slightly less than half. With such an increase, the South raised its gross share of the total United States income from 15 per cent in 1929 to 20 per cent in 1952.

Among the thirteen Southern states, Florida, Texas, and Virginia have usually been in the first position in the listing of the states by per capita incomes, and Alabama, Arkansas, Mississippi, and South Carolina have regularly shared the bottom positions on the list. Despite the significant gains in the Southern states, these states as a group remained clustered near the bottom of the states when ranked according to income. Nonetheless, there has been a narrowing of interstate differences both within the Southern region and within the nation as a whole.

Within states income differentials appear according to rural and urban places of residence and according to race, but recent trends indicate that the ranges are being narrowed. In 1949 the median income for all persons in the South was $1,367. For farm persons the median was $787 and for non-farm persons, $1,572. For non-white persons the median was $739 and for white persons, $1,647. The United States median was $1,917. Differentials between Southern farm persons and non-farm persons and between Southern white

TABLE 51

Per Capita Annual Income Payments in South and Non-South in Current Dollars and as a Percentage of 1929 and South as a Percentage of Non-South, 1929-1952

[*Figures given in current dollars*]

Year	Amount		Index		South as Percentage of Non-South
	South	Non-South	South	Non-South	
1929	372	797	100	100	46.7
1930	302	707	81	89	42.7
1931	251	594	67	75	42.3
1932	203	448	55	56	45.3
1933	208	430	56	54	48.4
1934	249	485	67	61	51.3
1935	272	533	73	67	51.0
1936	314	615	84	77	51.0
1937	331	650	89	82	50.9
1938	307	587	83	74	52.3
1939	322	624	87	78	51.6
1940	340	667	91	84	51.0
1941	423	800	114	100	52.9
1942	568	998	153	125	56.9
1943	715	1198	192	150	59.7
1944	815	1298	219	163	62.8
1945	849	1325	228	166	64.1
1946	855	1352	230	170	63.2
1947	951	1456	256	183	65.3
1948	1005	1561	270	196	64.4
1949	954	1464	256	184	65.2
1950	1025	1597	276	200	64.2
1951	1144	1746	308	219	65.5
1952	1199	1811	322	227	66.2

Source: U.S. Department of Commerce, Income Division, *Survey of Current Business*, August, 1953.

persons and non-white persons are larger for the South than for the other major regions of the United States.

Thus Table 51 depicts the achievement of an economic New South, with greatly improved capacity to pay for adequate schools for its growing population.

THE SHIFTING SOURCES OF INCOME

The income to individuals in the South has grown at a faster rate than that of the non-South since 1929. The analysis of the changing sources of the South's income is basic to understanding how this growth has come about and why it has occurred recently in the South.

The sources of income of particular significance in portraying the change are agriculture, manufacturing, and government. In 1929 the South was deriving one-fifth of its income from agriculture, one-eight of its income from manufacturing activities, and only one-twelfth from government sources. But by 1952 agriculture as a source had been cut in half, manufacturing had increased by half, and government had increased two and one-half times. In the non-South, by contrast, agriculture as a source decreased only one-third, manufacturing increased less than one-third, and government only twice. In both the South and the non-South, the changes in trades and services and other sources of income were less dramatic, although there were substantial decreases in the non-South from other sources of income in the quarter century.

The declining role of Southern agriculture as a source of income is associated with the urban trend in the South, with changing patterns of agriculture, and the depopulation of the farm South. Farming, particularly cotton farming, was for sixty-five years the keystone of both the economic and social structure to which the values and attitudes regarding Negroes were basically related. After 1930 income from agriculture as a percentage of total income in the region sharply declined. The present agricultural patterns are both less exploitative and more productive; the number of people engaged in farming has decreased impressively and the dominant culture has undergone a transformation, including new demands for schooling.

The increases in manufacturing income reflect great gains in the production of goods for the expanding home market as well as for the national market. Increases are accounted for not only by expansion of the kinds of manufacturing traditionally based in the South, such as textiles, but also by many new types. In recent years, manufacturing expansion has been particularly marked in production processes involving large amounts of capital outlay. Some of the new expansion is accounted for by the gains accruing to the South from war industry, but the South did not gain in this area as significantly as did other parts of the nation. The industrial growth is more accurately explained in terms of the market opportunities, the resources available for development, the large labor force, and the low comparative costs.

The increases in government expenditures came at all levels, local, state, and federal. Economists see little prospect for any substantial net decline in the total government expenditures in the near future.

The shift from manufacturing in which the value added is low to more complex industrial processes is significant in terms of the kind of workers required and the kind of schools needed for their education. With the changes in sources of income have come occupational changes; there are fewer farm workers and unskilled workers and more professionals, non-farm proprietors, clerks, and sales workers, skilled workers, and semi-skilled workers.

In short, Table 52 gives a statistical measure of the economic growth of the South and of the movement toward the norms achieved earlier in other regions.

[101]

TABLE 52
Income Payments to Individuals by Components as Percentage of Total Income and Percentage Change for United States and Southern States, 1929 and 1952

	Agricultural Income			Manufacturing Payrolls		
	1929	1952	Change from 1929 to 1952	1929	1952	Change from 1929 to 1952
United States.........	8.4	6.7	− 1.7	19.7	24.5	+4.8
Alabama...........	22.0	10.0	−12.0	16.0	20.6	+4.6
Arkansas..........	30.7	22.0	− 8.7	9.1	11.9	+2.8
Florida............	9.9	7.5	− 2.4	10.8	8.1	−2.7
Georgia...........	20.9	9.5	−11.4	15.6	20.1	+4.5
Kentucky..........	20.5	11.9	− 8.6	11.1	14.8	+3.7
Louisiana..........	16.7	9.4	− 7.3	14.1	14.4	+0.3
Mississippi........	38.9	24.1	−14.8	10.3	12.5	+2.2
N. Carolina........	20.4	15.4	− 5.0	21.3	25.8	+4.5
Oklahoma.........	18.5	11.6	− 6.9	6.8	10.2	+3.4
S. Carolina........	24.3	11.0	−13.3	19.7	24.2	+4.5
Tennessee.........	19.1	9.6	− 9.5	16.1	24.4	+6.3
Texas.............	20.2	10.6	− 9.6	8.3	13.0	+4.7
Virginia...........	15.0	7.9	− 7.1	14.3	17.3	+3.0

	Trade and Service Income			Governmental Income Payments			Other Income		
	1929	1952	Change from 1929 to 1952	1929	1952	Change from 1929 to 1952	1929	1952	Change from 1929 to 1952
United States....	24.4	25.6	+1.2	7.3	15.9	+ 8.6	40.2	27.3	−12.9
Alabama......	22.8	23.7	+0.9	7.8	22.6	+14.8	31.4	23.1	− 8.3
Arkansas.....	25.4	24.8	−0.6	8.3	18.3	+10.0	26.5	23.0	− 3.5
Florida.......	29.9	32.4	+2.5	10.1	20.2	+10.1	39.3	31.8	− 7.5
Georgia.......	27.4	26.5	−0.9	7.8	21.0	+13.2	28.3	22.9	− 5.4
Kentucky.....	21.9	23.4	+1.5	7.6	19.2	+11.6	38.9	30.7	− 8.2
Louisiana.....	24.7	24.5	−0.2	8.1	20.2	+12.1	36.4	31.5	− 4.9
Mississippi....	21.1	23.7	+2.6	8.6	21.1	+12.5	21.1	18.6	− 2.5
N. Carolina...	23.0	22.9	−0.1	8.3	16.1	+ 7.8	27.0	19.8	− 7.2
Oklahoma.....	23.5	24.6	+1.1	7.5	21.9	+14.4	43.7	31.7	−12.0
S. Carolina....	24.9	20.4	−4.5	10.3	19.7	+ 9.4	20.8	24.7	+ 3.9
Tennessee.....	26.1	25.4	−0.8	8.0	18.0	+10.0	30.7	24.7	− 6.0
Texas........	25.5	26.3	+0.8	7.2	17.1	+ 9.9	38.8	30.0	− 5.8
Virginia......	25.1	23.5	−1.6	9.9	26.3	+16.4	35.8	25.0	−10.8

Source: U.S. Department of Commerce, Income Division, *Survey of Current Business*, August, 1953.

INCOME PROJECTIONS UNDER THE CONSERVATIVE ASSUMPTION

Two sets of income projections are made in this volume. The first yields conservative and the second optimistic estimates, or "lows" and "highs." These afford a range of expected income for each year. Basic to this range of expected income is the general economic assumption that the federal government under its monetary-fiscal policy will be successful in preventing a major business depression before the close of the decade. (The details of the method of projection are presented in Appendix 8.)

Total income in this study is defined as the sum of the payments to the factors of production—wages and salaries, rents and royalties, interest, and profits.

The conservative projections, the lows, are based on the assumption that the economic development of the South reached its highest rate by 1952 and that from 1952 it will fall off to a rate of growth around 3.2 per cent, the rate experienced before the intensification of industrialization and comparable to the rate of growth of the United States as a whole from 1890 to World War II.

These conservative, or low estimates, are shown in Table 53. All the data are stated in 1952 dollars. Income in the South is thus expected to reach $67.2 billions in 1960, an increase over 1952 of $16.2 billions, or 32 per cent.

Some states, of course, are expected to have a greater increase than are others; and such differences as arise may be attributable to the degree of transition from an agrarian to an industrial economy in each state. South Carolina may anticipate the highest gain of all the Southern states over the remainder of this decade, some 35 per cent. The percentage increases from 1952 to 1960 for the states in a descending order are: South Carolina, 34.8; Texas, 34.5; Florida, 34.1; Georgia, 32.5; Tennessee, 32.4; Alabama, 32.2; North Carolina, 31.8; Virginia, 30.9; Kentucky, 30.3; Louisiana, 29.4; Arkansas and Mississippi, 27.8; and Oklahoma, 27.6.

Although the income increase for Oklahoma is the lowest, it probably reflects the conditions of the period covered in the pro-

TABLE 53

Total Income Payment Projections for South and Southern States Under the Conservative Assumption, 1953-1960

[*Figures given to nearest billion of 1952 dollars*]

	YEARS								
	1952*	1953	1954	1955	1956	1957	1958	1959	1960
South	51.0†	53.0	55.0	57.0	59.1	61.1	63.1	65.2	67.2
Alabama	3.1	3.2	3.3	3.5	3.6	3.7	3.8	3.9	4.1
Arkansas	1.8	1.9	1.9	2.0	2.1	2.1	2.2	2.3	2.3
Florida	4.1	4.3	4.4	4.6	4.8	5.0	5.2	5.3	5.5
Georgia	4.0	4.2	4.3	4.5	4.6	4.8	5.0	5.1	5.3
Kentucky	3.3	3.4	3.6	3.7	3.8	3.9	4.1	4.2	4.3
Louisiana	3.4	3.5	3.7	3.8	3.9	4.0	4.2	4.3	4.4
Mississippi	1.8	1.8	1.9	2.0	2.0	2.1	2.2	2.2	2.3
N. Carolina	4.4	4.6	4.7	4.9	5.1	5.3	5.4	5.6	5.8
Oklahoma	2.9	3.0	3.1	3.2	3.3	3.4	3.5	3.6	3.7
S. Carolina	2.3	2.4	2.5	2.6	2.7	2.8	2.9	3.0	3.1
Tennessee	3.7	3.8	4.0	4.1	4.3	4.4	4.6	4.7	4.9
Texas	11.9	12.4	13.0	13.4	14.0	14.5	15.0	15.5	16.0
Virginia	4.3	4.5	4.6	4.8	4.9	5.1	5.3	5.4	5.6

*1952 data are actual.
†Data may not add to totals due to rounding.

jections, 1938 and 1939. Oklahoma, industrially being primarily a crude-oil producing and refining state, had recovered by 1938 from the depths of the depression to a somewhat higher level of economic activity than had many of the other Southern states; hence the trend line was tipped downward a bit by the relatively high incomes of the late 1930's.

The high income increase anticipated for Florida is the product more of its growing tourist trade than of industrialization, although some drift away from agricultural activity is to be noted.

INCOME PROJECTIONS UNDER THE OPTIMISTIC ASSUMPTION

The second income projection rests on the assumption that the Southern economy will enjoy an intensified rate of industrialization, instead of dropping toward the pre-war national rate. This assumption yields a series of "high" income estimates for the South and the Southern states. Again, it must be assumed that there will be no major decline in business activity.

In the computation of this income series, two fundamental methodological propositions are involved. (They are developed in detail in Appendix 8.) First, per capita incomes are projected, 1953 to 1960. The use of per capita income for the purpose of income projection is quite tenable; changes in population are thus adjusted so that a better measure of the rate of changes in income is obtained. Second, per capita data are reconverted into total income figures.

The results of the first step are summarized in Table 54 which gives the per capita income projections by states for 1953-1960, stated in 1952 dollars. The forecast for each state goes out from the proposition that the rate of income growth actually experienced by each state during the period 1938-1952 will be repeated in the remainder of the 1950's decade. These annual rates of growth stated as percentages and with the states in descending order are: South Carolina, 6.52; Mississippi, 6.27; Alabama, 6.15; Georgia, 5.64; Arkansas, 5.59; Tennessee, 5.57; Kentucky, 5.54; Oklahoma, 5.41; Texas, 5.05; North Carolina, 4.80; Louisiana, 4.62; Virginia, 4.49; and Florida, 3.75. Florida is now at the bottom since its rate of growth up to and including 1938 had been at a somewhat higher level than those for other states; therefore the base figure tends to pull down the projections. In a similar position are Louisiana and Virginia.

In actual per capita figures, Texas may look forward to the highest 1960 income, $2,151, of the Southern states. Oklahoma, with a per capita income of $1,956 in 1960, is next. Mississippi, although it has experienced a very high rate of income growth since 1938, is still lowest of all the Southern states with its income of $1,330. Arkansas lies next above with an income of $1,468. The difference between $2,151 to $1,330, or $821, is highly significant and demonstrates the impact of industrialization.

The results of the reconversion of per capita income payments into total income payments are tabulated in Table 55. Income for the South, by this method, will reach 85 billions in 1960, an increase of $34.1 billions, or 66.9 per cent since 1952. As in the case of per capita income, Texas with $20.5 billions of total income is the highest. Next in line is Florida with $7.5 billions. Arkansas' $2.7 billions is the lowest.

TABLE 54
Per Capita Income for Southern States Projected by High Income Assumption for 1953-1960

[*Figures given in 1952 dollars*]

	1952*	1953	1954	1955	1956	1957	1958	1959	1960
Alabama	1,012	1,074	1,140	1,210	1,285	1,364	1,448	1,537	1,630
Arkansas	951	1,004	1,060	1,120	1,182	1,248	1,318	1,392	1,468
Florida	1,319	1,368	1,420	1,473	1,528	1,586	1,645	1,707	1,770
Georgia	1,137	1,201	1,269	1,340	1,416	1,496	1,580	1,669	1,762
Kentucky	1,135	1,198	1,264	1,334	1,408	1,486	1,569	1,655	1,747
Louisiana	1,206	1,262	1,320	1,381	1,445	1,512	1,581	1,654	1,734
Mississippi	818	869	924	982	1,043	1,109	1,178	1,252	1,330
N. Carolina	1,049	1,099	1,152	1,207	1,265	1,326	1,390	1,456	1,525
Oklahoma	1,285	1,355	1,438	1,505	1,586	1,672	1,763	1,858	1,956
S. Carolina	1,099	1,171	1,247	1,328	1,415	1,507	1,605	1,710	1,821
Tennessee	1,126	1,189	1,255	1,325	1,399	1,477	1,559	1,646	1,740
Texas	1,452	1,525	1,602	1,683	1,768	1,858	1,951	2,050	2,151
Virginia	1,322	1,381	1,443	1,508	1,576	1,647	1,721	1,798	1,878

*1952 data are actual.

TABLE 55
1952 Total Income Payments and Projected High Total Income Payments for South and Southern States, 1953-1960

[*Figures given to nearest millions of 1952 dollars*]

	1952	1953	1954	1955	1956	1957	1958	1959	1960
South	50,957	54,328	57,922	61,753	65,838	70,193	74,837	79,787	85,065
Alabama	3,089	3,299	3,524	3,764	4,021	4,295	4,587	4,900	5,234
Arkansas	1,785	1,881	1,982	2,089	2,201	2,319	2,444	2,575	2,714
Florida	4,088	4,410	4,758	5,133	5,537	5,974	6,445	6,953	7,501
Georgia	3,998	4,264	4,547	4,850	5,172	5,516	5,883	6,274	6,691
Kentucky	3,311	3,505	3,710	3,927	4,157	4,400	4,658	4,930	5,219
Louisiana	3,396	3,603	3,822	4,054	4,301	4,563	4,840	5,135	5,447
Mississippi	1,778	1,891	2,011	2,138	2,274	2,418	2,572	2,735	2,908
N. Carolina	4,383	4,652	4,938	5,241	5,563	5,904	6,267	6,652	7,060
Oklahoma	2,910	3,059	3,217	3,382	3,555	3,738	3,930	4,132	4,344
S. Carolina	2,341	2,517	2,706	2,910	3,129	3,364	3,618	3,890	4,182
Tennessee	3,669	3,910	4,166	4,439	4,730	5,040	5,371	5,723	6,098
Texas	11,887	12,723	13,618	14,576	15,602	16,699	17,874	19,132	20,478
Virginia	4,322	4,607	4,911	5,235	5,581	5,949	6,342	6,761	7,207

A COMPARISON OF THE LOW AND HIGH INCOME PROJECTIONS AND THEIR CAPACITY FOR MEETING FISCAL NEEDS

A comparison of the 1960 income projections by the conservative and optimistic assumptions portrays the range of incomes obtained from the two projections. The difference between these figures is the estimate of the range of income available for meeting the fiscal needs of the expanded educational program outlined above. Generally speaking, what applies to 1960 will apply to the entire series of years, 1953 to 1960, for the region and for each state.

The difference for the South as a whole is $18 billions. For the thirteen states, the average difference between the low and high estimates is $1.4 billion. The variation among states is significant. Apparently the lowest differences exist where the process of industrialization has yet to be achieved; the high differences are associated, as a rule, with the states where industrialization is moving ahead. Texas, now rapidly becoming one of the major producers of certain chemicals, shows the greatest spread between the two income estimates. Moving from an economy largely in a primary stage of economic development—farming, ranching, and extractive activities—to an economy of a secondary stage—manufacturing and raw materials conversion—its growth of income under the optimistic assumption places it among the high income states of the region.

By allocation of a portion of each year's income, low and high levels, to education, an area within which the yearly educational costs may range is found. Thus, for the region, an allocation of 3.3 per cent income at each level gives a potential range of school funds from $2.2 billions to $2.8 billions in 1960. More about this ratio will be said in the next chapter. Although expenditures at the upper limit of the range would provide relatively good public schools, the region's educational expenditures may well exceed this theoretical upper limit of its capacity to pay. To be sure, there is no lower limit, for the people of a state could dispense entirely with public education if they so desired. But to spend less than $2.2 billions would suggest that by no means the best possible efforts were being put forth on the behalf of the children of the South.

A number of Southern states are now spending at a ratio higher than the upper limit assumes. That other public services are suffering because of these efforts may or may not be the case; in any event, the latter issue appears to have been set aside until education is advanced somewhat in line with the economic requirements of the New South.

TABLE 56

Projected Total "High" Income Payments for South and Southern States Derived from the Per Capita Income for 1960 and Compared with Projected "Low" Income Payments

[*Figures given to nearest billion of 1952 dollars*]

	Projected Total "Low" Income Payments	Projected Total "High" Income Payments	Difference
South	$67.3	$85.0	$17.7
Alabama	4.1	5.2	1.1
Arkansas	2.3	2.7	0.4
Florida	5.5	7.5	2.0
Georgia	5.3	6.7	1.4
Kentucky	4.3	5.2	0.9
Louisiana	4.4	5.4	1.0
Mississippi	2.3	2.9	0.6
N. Carolina	5.8	7.1	1.3
Oklahoma	3.7	4.3	0.6
S. Carolina	3.1	4.2	1.1
Tennessee	4.9	6.1	1.2
Texas	16.0	20.5	4.5
Virginia	5.6	7.2	1.6

Chapter 9

The South's Ability to Pay

TOTAL COSTS OF EQUALIZATION AND IMPROVEMENT AND OF PROVIDING FOR THE RISE IN AVERAGE DAILY ATTENDANCE

The question to be answered in this chapter is whether the South can afford the program outlined in the preceding chapters. In summary, the program involves providing for: (1) the costs of equalization across the board; (2) the capital deficit as of 1952; (3) the increase in current expenditures and transportation to meet the yearly growth in average daily attendance; and (4) the increase in plant and equipment outlay to accommodate the growth in enrollment.

The first step in focusing upon this question is to bring together the current and transportation costs and to note what is involved in their projection.

In 1951-52, the total current costs were $1,226,000,000 for the South. This sum includes the expenditures for administration or general control, instruction, plant operation and maintenance, a miscellany of expenses, and transportation. For reasons already stated, transportation costs have been excluded in the equalization computations; but since they must be included in the total cost summary, they are to be combined with the operating and instructional costs. This combining is first treated in Table 57 which shows the sum of the actual total current and transportation expenditures, the costs of equalization, and the annual cost to meet increments in average daily attendance. This table simply shows the data basic to the computation of total costs. Thus, to equalize the current expenditures across the board, the costs of equalization would be added to the 1951-52 total of current and transportation expenditures.

Oklahoma, already having equalized at a figure well above the goal of $166 per pupil in average daily attendance, will have no equalization expenditures to make. But, like all the states, it must make provision for the growth in average daily attendance. This annual cost figure for Oklahoma is $1,363,000.

For the South as a region, the total cost of equalization is $209,590,000 and the annual cost for increase in average daily attendance, $49,968,000. Once the current expenditures have been equalized ac-

TABLE 57

Total 1951-52 Current and Transportation Expenditures, the Costs of Equalization as of 1951-52 Across the Board, and the Annual Costs for Increments in Average Daily Attendance and Transportation for South and Southern States

[*Figures given to nearest $1,000*]

	Total 1951-52 Current and Transportation Expenditures	The Costs of Equalization	Annual Increments
South............	$1,226,000	$209,590	$49,968
Alabama.........	75,545	27,650	2,697
Arkansas........	37,125	25,280	1,667
Florida..........	88,579	4,750	3,589
Georgia..........	107,465	12,270	4,757
Kentucky........	70,620	13,610	2,705
Louisiana........	96,508	13,690	3,940
Mississippi.......	42,068	41,740	1,643
N. Carolina......	125,034	16,940	3,307
Oklahoma........	84,028	—	1,363
S. Carolina......	58,414	14,460	2,893
Tennessee........	85,123	19,720	2,925
Texas...........	268,023	9,030	14,658
Virginia.........	87,675	10,450	3,824

cording to the goal assumed here, the only annual addition is that to provide for growth in average daily attendance. This yearly increment is cumulative, and each yearly addition is added to the last.

In other words, once the base figure including transportation and equalized current expenditures is derived, the cost for each succeeding year is obtained by the addition of the annual attendance increment costs for the state or region. By this process not only equalization is provided but also improvement for the pupils of 1951-52 as well as those in years to come.

PROJECTION OF CURRENT AND TRANSPORTATION EXPENDITURES, 1952-53 TO 1959-60

The projection of the current and transportation expenditures is based upon the data summarized in Table 57. Starting with the total of actual current and transportation expenditures in 1951-52, the costs of equalization are added to give the total of equalized current expenditures plus transportation for 1951-52. For each year from then on, the annual increment to provide equalized expenditures and transportation for the annual growth in average daily attendance is accumulated.

Consider the projection for the state of Alabama. The actual total current and transportation expenditure in 1951-52 was $75,545,000. To this figure is added $27,650,000, the cost of equalization of current expenditures for this state, and the sum represents equalized current expenditures plus transportation. Next is added $2,697,000, to provide for one year's growth in ADA. The total gives the projected costs of equalized current expenditure plus transportation for 1952-53, or a total of $105,892,000. For 1953-54, the projected value is $105,892,000 plus $2,697,000, or $108,589,000; for 1954-55, it is $108,589,000 plus $2,697,000; and so on for the remaining years through 1959-60. For the South and for each of the thirteen states, Table 58 brings together the projected equalized current expenditures and transportation expenditures for each of the eight years.

The total current and transportation expenses for the region are expected to increase 33 per cent by 1960. The percentage increase for the region and the states will be affected by both the dollar per pupil equalization gap and the increment of average daily attendance. Some states will have large increases percentagewise because of a large gap which must be filled to effect equalization, while the increment in average daily attendance may be relatively low. Others may be faced with the opposite condition, small gap but large attendance increment.

The state increases from 1951-52 to 1959-60 percentagewise, in descending order, are: Texas, 42.3; Georgia, 31.8; South Carolina, 31.7; Virginia, 31.2; Florida, 30.7; Louisiana, 28.6; Kentucky, 25.8; Tennessee, 22.3; Arkansas, 21.3; Alabama, 20.9; North Carolina, 18.6; Mississippi, 15.8; and Oklahoma, 13.0.

TABLE 58

Projection of Current and Transportation Expenditures for South and Southern States, 1952-1960

[Figures given to nearest million of dollars]

	1951-52	1952-53	1953-54	1954-55	1955-56	1956-57	1957-58	1958-59	1959-60
South	$1,435.8	$1,485.8	$1,535.7	$1,585.7	$1,635.7	$1,685.6	$1,735.6	$1,785.6	$1,835.5
Alabama	103.2	105.9	108.6	111.3	114.0	116.7	119.4	122.1	124.8
Arkansas	62.4	64.1	65.7	67.4	69.1	70.7	72.4	74.1	75.7
Florida	93.3	96.9	100.5	104.1	107.7	111.3	114.9	118.5	122.0
Georgia	119.7	124.5	129.2	134.0	138.8	143.5	148.3	153.0	157.8
Kentucky	84.2	86.9	89.6	92.3	95.1	97.8	100.5	103.2	105.9
Louisiana	110.2	114.1	118.1	122.0	126.0	129.9	133.8	137.8	141.7
Mississippi	83.8	85.5	87.1	88.7	90.4	92.0	93.7	95.3	97.0
N. Carolina	142.0	145.3	148.6	151.9	155.2	158.5	161.8	165.1	168.4
Oklahoma	84.0	85.4	86.8	88.1	89.5	90.8	92.2	93.6	94.9
S. Carolina	72.9	75.8	78.7	81.6	84.4	87.3	90.2	93.1	96.0
Tennessee	104.8	107.8	110.7	113.6	116.5	119.5	122.4	125.3	128.2
Texas	277.1	291.7	306.4	321.0	335.7	350.3	365.0	379.7	394.3
Virginia	98.1	101.9	105.8	109.6	113.4	117.2	121.1	124.9	128.7

FUNDING AND AMORTIZING THE CAPITAL DEFICIT

As seen in Table 47 the Southern states in 1951-52 had sizable capital deficits—the differences between the 1951-52 value of buildings and equipment and the cost of adequate buildings and equipment. Most states could not possibly meet the capital deficits out of the current revenues of 1953. For that reason, the financing of the deficit by bond flotation is assumed; funds are thus made immediately available without too serious a drain on the state treasuries, and the improvement of educational program is accelerated.

Funding the deficit into twenty-five-year bonds bearing 3 per cent interest seems entirely feasible. A longer period than twenty-five years might have been selected, but the retirement of debt in this time makes possible the replacement of the buildings in not too distant a future so that the public schools will be fairly continuously modernized. The 3 per cent rate is the approximate average of the actual rates at which bond financing has been taking place in the national long-term money market. Although a number of Southern states have been financing at rates less than 3 per cent, this figure is a reasonable choice.

Table 59 presents the amortization payments and the accounting for the interest. The figures are for the region, but the procedure is the same for each state. In the first period a total debt of $1,928 millions is incurred through the sale of a twenty-five-year bond issue at 3 per cent interest. The annual payment made will amount to $110.7 millions. Of this amount, a decreasing portion is applied to interest and an increasing portion is applied to pay off the principal. These computations are based on the usual interest and amortization formula and need not be developed here.

In the first year of the annual payment of $110.7 millions, $57.8 millions go to cover interest and $52.9 millions to reduce the principal. By the twenty-fifth year only $108 millions of the principal remains so that the payment in that year covers $3.2 millions of interest and $107.5 millions of debt. The figures are not precise because of the rounding-off to one decimal place.

The annual amortization payments for the thirteen states in millions of dollars are as follows: Alabama, 11.3; Arkansas, 8.1; Florida, 3.7; Georgia, 7.1; Kentucky, 10.7; Louisiana, 6.0; Mississippi, 7.1; North Carolina, 13.8; Oklahoma, 5.7; South Carolina, 5.6; Tennessee, 12.9; Texas, 10.2; and Virginia, 8.5.

TABLE 59

Amortization of Capital Deficit of $1,928 Millions Over a Twenty-Five Year Term at 3 Per Cent

[*Figures given to nearest million dollars*]

Period	Principal Balance Beginning of Period	Total Annual Payment	Applied to Interest	Applied to Principal
1	$1,928.0	$110.7	$57.8	$52.9
2	1,875.1	110.7	56.3	54.4
3	1,820.7	110.7	54.6	56.1
4	1,764.6	110.7	52.9	57.8
5	1,706.8	110.7	51.2	59.5
6	1,647.3	110.7	49.4	61.3
7	1,586.0	110.7	47.6	63.1
8	1,522.9	110.7	45.7	65.0
9	1,457.9	110.7	43.7	67.0
10	1,390.9	110.7	41.7	69.0
11	1,321.9	110.7	39.7	71.0
12	1,250.9	110.7	37.5	73.2
13	1,177.7	110.7	35.3	75.4
14	1,102.3	110.7	33.1	77.6
15	1,024.7	110.7	30.7	80.0
16	944.7	110.7	28.3	82.4
17	862.3	110.7	25.9	84.8
18	777.5	110.7	23.3	87.4
19	690.1	110.7	20.7	90.0
20	600.1	110.7	18.0	92.7
21	507.4	110.7	15.2	95.5
22	411.9	110.7	12.4	98.3
23	313.6	110.7	9.4	101.3
24	212.3	110.7	6.4	104.3
25	108.0	110.7	3.2	107.5

CAPITAL DEFICITS AND THEIR AMORTIZATION IN THE SOUTH AND BY STATES

The yearly amortization costs required in the funding of the capital deficits for the region and for each state are compiled in Table 60. The first column gives the total capital deficit by region and by state; the second, the annual amortization payment which, as explained above under Table 59, comprises annual interest and principal payments.

Through funding of the capital deficit, its annual burden is reduced to the payments for amortization and interest. Thus, Alabama's total capital deficit is $196,000,000; but by funding the capital deficit can be converted into a yearly cost of $11,300,000. Hence, the individual states can go far in early improvement of their school systems through the means of long-term financing. The new plant and equipment are made available immediately.

TABLE 60

Capital Deficits and Annual Amortization Payments for South and Southern States, 1951-52

[*Figures given to nearest million of dollars*]

	Capital Deficits	Annual Amortization Payments
South	$1,928	$110.7
Alabama	196	11.3
Arkansas	141	8.1
Florida	65	3.7
Georgia	124	7.1
Kentucky	186	10.7
Louisiana	104	6.0
Mississippi	123	7.1
N. Carolina	241	13.8
Oklahoma	100	5.7
S. Carolina	98	5.6
Tennessee	225	12.9
Texas	177	10.2
Virginia	148	8.5

THE GROWTH IN ENROLLMENT AND THE ADDITIONAL CAPITAL NEEDS

Not only must a sizable capital deficit related to the pupils in school in 1951-52 be met, but, in addition, the growth in enrollment also necessitates further outlays for plant and equipment for the years 1953 through 1960. These annual capital outlay figures are shown in Table 61.

The year-by-year increase in enrollment would govern this cost. Over the eight-year period, 1953-60, the total needs for the region are estimated at $1,296,000,000. On the assumption that the rise in enrollment will be by approximately constant yearly amounts, the total outlay is divided by eight to give annual amounts. (Appendix 6 outlines the method used in estimating these needs.) For the total region, this yearly increment in plant and equipment is expected to run around $162,000,000. By states it will of course be significantly smaller. It ranges all the way from $5,430,000 for Oklahoma to $41,572,000 a year for Texas.

TABLE 61

Annual Capital Outlay to Meet School Enrollment Growth in South and Southern States, 1952-1960

[*Figures given to nearest $1,000*]

	Outlay
South	$161,891
Alabama	8,048
Arkansas	6,277
Florida	8,860
Georgia	11,887
Kentucky	11,486
Louisiana	11,180
Mississippi	7,014
N. Carolina	15,410
Oklahoma	5,430
S. Carolina	7,974
Tennessee	12,112
Texas	41,572
Virginia	14,632

THE FISCAL NEEDS—AN EXAMPLE OF ACCOUNTING FOR THE COSTS

The next step is to account for all the proposed expenditures. An important assumption is involved: as already indicated above, the capital deficits will not be financed out of current income but by bond issues. In Table 62, therefore, the yearly retirement of debt and payments of interest are applied as "expense," while the actual outlay to meet the costs of the deficit plant and equipment is not entered. In a sense this procedure is tantamount to the incurring of an expense but only loosely so. Were the states to prepare a capital budget as distinct from a current budget, then a proper separation of administration, instructional, and operating expenses from capital outlays could be made. Lacking this separation, the nearest approach to it is the process developed in Table 62.

The total current expenditures plus transportation in 1951-52, the base year, are $1,226 million. The cost of equalization across the board, i.e., for both Negro and white pupils and for districts within the states up to the criteria already stated, is $210 million. (See Table 57 above.) The yearly amortization of the capital deficit on a funded basis rounded off is $111,000,000. (See Table 59 above.) The annual capital outlay needed to meet the growth in enrollment rounded off is $162,000,000. (See Table 61 above.) These four figures together are added to derive the "base" expenditures of $1,709,000,000. This total provides for: (1) equalization of current expenditures; (2) for the capital deficit which also equalizes the plant and equipment for all pupils, Negro and white, as of 1951-52; and (3) for the annual growth in capital to meet the yearly increases in enrollment by 1959-60. These increases are assumed to be linear.

But this sum does not provide for the cumulative growth in equalized current expenditures plus transportation. There must be accumulated year by year an amount of $50,000,000 to cover this need. (See Table 57 above.) Hence the total fiscal requirements in 1952-53 will reach $1,759,000,000 for the South. The total fiscal needs in 1953-54 will be $1,759,000,000 plus $50,000,000, or $1,809,000,000. The $50,000,000 is cumulative with each year so that by 1959-60 equalized current expenditures plus transportation, because of the yearly growth in average daily attendance, will reach $1,836,000,000. The total costs, including capital deficit funding and the annual growth in capital, will reach in 1959-60, $2,109,000,000.

TABLE 62

Estimation of Fiscal Requirements to Meet Equalization Across the Board, Capital Deficits Funded, and the Growth in Capital and Current Needs in the South, 1951-1960

Total Current Expenditures in 1951-52 Including Transportation Costs	$1,226,000,000
Equalization Across the Board as of 1951-52	210,000,000
Capital Deficit Funded	111,000,000
Annual Capital Outlay to Meet Growth	162,000,000
Total "Base" Expenditures	$1,709,000,000
Annual Increment in Current and Transportation Costs	50,000,000
Total Expenditures, 1952-53	1,759,000,000

To derive the yearly costs for the period, simply accumulate $50,000,000 each year:

Year	Costs
1952-53	$1,759,000,000
1953-54	1,809,000,000
1954-55	1,859,000,000
1955-56	1,909,000,000
1956-57	1,959,000,000
1957-58	2,009,000,000
1958-59	2,059,000,000
1959-60	2,109,000,000

YEAR-BY-YEAR PROJECTION OF TOTAL COSTS, CURRENT, TRANSPORTATION, AND CAPITAL

The accounting process for the states, which is identical with that used for the region in the previous section, is illustrated by the following computation for the state of Alabama:

Equalized current expenditures plus transportation, 1951-52 (from Table 58)	$103,195,000
Capital deficit funded (from Table 60)	11,300,000
Annual capital outlay to meet growth (from Table 61)	8,048,000
Base year total	122,543,000
Add annual increment in current and transportation expenditures (from Table 57)	2,697,000
Total expenditures, 1952-53	125,240,000

The 1953-54 projected expenditures are the sum of the 1952-53 expenditures, $125,240,000 plus $2,697,000—a total of $127,937,000; and so on, for the eight years. This same procedure is carried through for each state for the fiscal years 1952-53 through 1959-60 in Table 63.

The total of all expenditures, equalized current, transportation, and equalized capital in 1960 for the region is $2,108,200,000. (See Table 62.) This total includes the increment in attendance costs, the capital deficit amortization, the annual capital costs for growth in enrollment, the equalized current expenditures, and the transportation costs.

The average increase in total costs for the thirteen states by 1960, over and above the equalized current expenditures and transportation costs of 1951-52, is $51.7 million. There seems to be no major reason why each state cannot meet such costs. Using the mean figure $51.7 million as representative of the total increase state by state, an increase, beyond the basic equalization costs to be incurred immediately, of one-eighth of $51.7 million, or $6.5 million, would be required annually. The tax increases necessary to defray such amounts should not be too punitive.

The total cost increase could be further reduced, state by state, by funding also the capital growth, as well as the capital deficit. Whether such a practice would be desirable depends upon the degree to which each political unit wishes to load itself down with debt. Obviously, the lower the rate of interest on the debt, the more debt the unit can bear.

TABLE 63

Projection of Total Outlays, Current, Transportation, and Capital, on the Assumption of Equalization Across the Board for South and Southern States, 1952-1960

[Figures given to nearest million of dollars]

	Base Year Total	1952-53	1953-54	1954-55	1955-56	1956-57	1957-58	1958-59	1959-60
South	$1,708.4	$1,758.4	$1,808.3	$1,858.3	$1,908.3	$1,958.3	$2,008.2	$2,058.2	$2,108.2
Alabama	122.5	125.2	127.9	130.6	133.3	136.0	138.7	141.4	144.1
Arkansas	76.8	78.4	80.1	81.8	83.4	85.1	86.8	88.4	90.1
Florida	105.9	109.5	113.1	116.7	120.3	123.9	127.5	131.0	134.6
Georgia	138.7	143.5	148.3	153.0	157.8	162.5	167.3	172.0	176.8
Kentucky	106.4	109.1	111.8	114.5	117.2	119.9	122.6	125.3	128.0
Louisiana	127.4	131.3	135.2	139.2	143.1	147.1	151.0	154.9	158.9
Mississippi	97.9	99.5	101.2	102.8	104.5	106.1	107.7	109.4	111.0
N. Carolina	171.2	174.5	177.8	181.1	184.5	187.8	191.1	194.4	197.7
Oklahoma	95.2	96.6	97.9	99.3	100.7	102.0	103.4	104.7	106.1
S. Carolina	86.5	89.4	92.3	95.2	98.0	100.9	103.8	106.7	109.6
Tennessee	129.9	132.8	135.7	138.7	141.6	144.5	147.4	150.4	153.3
Texas	328.8	343.4	358.1	372.8	387.4	402.1	416.7	431.4	446.1
Virginia	121.3	125.1	128.9	132.7	136.6	140.4	144.2	148.0	151.8

COMPARISON OF YEARLY TOTAL EXPENDITURES WITH THE YEARLY HIGH AND LOW INCOMES

The story told in the previous tables is far from complete; it does not give a definite evaluation of whether the South and the Southern states can afford the program proposed in this volume. Table 64 compares the total projected expenditures with projected high and low incomes available for educational purposes in each state.

In the measurement of the cost burden, the two income projections developed above may be converted into income available for education. During the last decade or more the South on the average has tended to spend around 3.3 per cent of its total income payments upon public school education. The expenditures included are current, transportation, and capital. The concern here is with the same total. For the fiscal years 1939-40 to 1951-52 such totals as a percentage of total income payments averaged 3.3 per cent. To be sure, some states fell a bit below this figure, and others were well above it. But on the assumption that those below it will want to spend at least at this level to provide good schools for their children, the 3.3 per cent figure was applied to each state's total income figures high and low for the eight years to derive the high and low available funds for schools. This provides a range of the capacity to bear the burden of the education program.

Table 64 shows for the region and for each state three rows of figures: the first is the high available income, the second is projected expenditures, and the third is low available income. For the region, in 1952-53, the first year of projection, the total costs exceed the low available income but lie below the high available income. But in the following year the total costs are covered by both incomes. By 1959-60 the total costs are significantly less than either of the incomes.

For the states the results are generally promising. From the beginning of the period five of the states will be able to defray their projected total costs under either income condition. These states are Florida, Kentucky, Oklahoma, Texas and Virginia. Tennessee reaches a point where it almost breaks even in 1955-56, under its low income projection. In that fiscal year expenditures are $141,576,000 and income, $141,100,000, a shade under the required amount. Relative to its high income projections, it may be expected to reach the break-even point in 1953-54, with expenditures at $135,726,000 and income available for the expenditures, $137,500,000.

By 1960 twelve of the states will be able to meet all expenditures under the high income estimate. Of these twelve Arkansas barely gets under the wire, but its income in 1959-60 is close enough to

TABLE 64
Low and High Available Income and Total School Expenditures, 1952-53 through 1959-60

[*Figures given to nearest million of dollars*]

	1952-53	1953-54	1954-55	1955-56	1956-57	1957-58	1958-59	1959-60
South*								
High Income......	$1,792.6	$1,911.0	$2,037.4	$2,172.2	$2,315.9	$2,469.4	$2,633.1	$2,807.7
Expenditures.....	1,758.4	1,808.3	1,858.3	1,908.3	1,958.3	2,008.2	2,058.2	2,108.2
Low Income......	1,748.6	1,815.6	1,882.6	1,950.0	2,016.6	2,083.7	2,150.6	2,217.6
Alabama								
High Income..	108.9	116.3	124.2	132.7	141.7	151.4	161.7	172.7
Expenditures..	125.2	127.9	130.6	133.3	136.0	138.7	141.4	144.1
Low Income..	105.9	109.4	113.9	117.9	121.9	125.9	129.9	133.9
Arkansas								
High Income..	62.1	65.4	68.9	72.6	76.5	80.7	85.0	89.6
Expenditures..	78.4	80.1	81.8	83.4	85.1	86.8	88.4	90.1
Low Income..	61.1	63.3	65.5	67.7	69.8	72.1	74.3	76.5
Florida								
High Income..	145.5	157.0	169.4	182.7	197.1	212.7	229.4	247.5
Expenditures..	109.5	113.1	116.7	120.3	123.9	127.5	131.0	134.6
Low Income..	140.8	146.7	152.6	158.5	164.4	170.3	176.2	182.0
Georgia								
High Income..	140.7	150.1	160.0	170.7	182.0	194.1	207.0	220.8
Expenditures..	143.5	148.3	153.0	157.8	162.5	167.3	172.0	176.8
Low Income..	137.2	142.5	147.8	153.1	158.3	163.7	168.9	174.2
Kentucky								
High Income..	115.7	122.4	129.6	137.2	145.2	153.7	162.7	172.2
Expenditures..	109.1	111.8	114.5	117.2	119.9	122.6	125.3	128.0
Low Income..	113.4	117.4	121.5	125.7	129.7	133.8	137.7	142.0
Louisiana								
High Income..	118.9	126.1	133.8	141.9	150.6	159.7	169.5	179.8
Expenditures..	131.3	135.2	139.2	143.1	147.1	151.0	154.9	158.9
Low Income..	116.3	120.5	124.7	128.9	133.1	137.3	141.4	145.6
Mississippi								
High Income..	62.4	66.4	70.6	75.0	79.8	84.9	90.3	96.0
Expenditures..	99.5	101.2	102.8	104.5	106.1	107.7	109.4	111.0
Low Income..	60.9	63.1	65.3	67.5	69.6	71.9	74.1	76.2
N. Carolina								
High Income..	153.5	163.0	173.0	183.6	194.8	206.8	219.5	233.0
Expenditures..	174.5	177.8	181.1	184.5	187.8	191.1	194.4	197.7
Low Income..	150.5	156.3	162.1	167.9	173.7	179.6	185.5	191.4
Oklahoma								
High Income..	100.9	106.2	111.6	117.3	123.3	129.7	136.4	143.4
Expenditures..	96.6	97.9	99.3	100.7	102.0	103.4	104.7	106.1
Low Income..	99.3	102.5	105.6	108.9	112.1	115.3	118.6	121.8
S. Carolina								
High Income..	83.1	89.3	96.0	103.3	111.0	119.4	128.4	130.8
Expenditures..	89.4	92.3	95.2	98.0	100.9	103.8	106.7	109.6
Low Income..	80.3	83.2	86.3	89.3	92.3	95.2	98.2	101.2
Tennessee								
High Income..	129.0	137.5	146.5	156.1	166.3	177.2	188.9	201.2
Expenditures..	132.8	135.7	138.7	141.6	144.5	147.4	150.4	153.3
Low Income..	126.1	131.1	136.1	141.1	146.1	151.1	156.1	161.0
Texas								
High Income..	419.9	449.4	481.0	514.9	551.1	589.8	631.4	675.8
Expenditures..	343.4	358.1	372.8	387.4	402.1	416.7	431.4	446.1
Low Income..	409.2	426.2	443.2	460.2	477.2	494.2	511.1	528.0
Virginia								
High Income..	152.9	162.1	172.8	184.2	196.3	209.3	223.1	237.8
Expenditures..	125.1	128.9	132.7	136.6	140.4	144.2	148.0	151.8
Low Income..	147.8	153.0	158.2	163.3	168.5	173.6	178.8	183.9

*These totals will not agree with the totals found in Table 62 for the reason that they have been computed for each state, individually and separately; the totals in Table 62 were computed on a regional total basis.

warrant its inclusion in the group. Of these states, Georgia hits its break-even point in 1953-54 with expenditures of $148,257,000 and high income of $150,100,000. South Carolina's break-even point comes in the following year under the high income of $96,000,000 and expenditures of $95,155,000. Alabama, Louisiana, and North Carolina reach their break-even points in 1956-57. Mississippi is the only state which does not reach the goal by 1959-60. But, other conditions remaining the same, it may be expected to hit its break-even point around 1963-64 under the high income projection.

In the final analysis, therefore, the South, taken as a region, should encounter no great difficulty in financing an educational program consisting largely of the elements outlined in the previous chapters. The underlying assumption is, of course, that no truly significant declines in business activity and income will develop before the target year 1960 is reached. One or two states will encounter some difficulty but not of a magnitude to discourage them from going ahead with the program at least in its major aspects.

For those states more fortunate than others, in that they may have an excess or surplus or available income over total costs, there is the possibility of allocating these amounts to enrichment programs. Thus further improvement beyond that described here is possible for a number of the states.

Appendices

1. *The Selection of the Sample*

The sample data which are employed in this study were developed in the following fashion. The counties of the region were classified according to the degree of urbanization in 1950 and denominated as rural, rural-urban, and metropolitan. A rural county was one in which there was no urban population in 1950; a rural-urban county was one in which there was some urban population in 1950, but which did not fall into the census definition of metropolitan. A metropolitan county was one so classified by the census of 1950. When the counties of each state had been placed in their classification they were given a rank order in each classification by percentage of Negro population. The county with the highest percentage of Negro population in the classification for the state was placed at the top of the list and the next highest second until all the counties had been so placed. Then four counties in each of the rural and rural-urban classifications were chosen by taking a county at or near the median of each fourth of the distribution. A map of the state was consulted to see that each important geographical area had representation in the sample. If two of the counties in the same sample were in the same geographical area, another county near the median of the fourth of the distribution in which one of these counties fell was selected. By such a method the sample of the classification included four counties representative of the range of Negro population of the geographical distribution of counties in that classification for the state. Thus a directed sample of rural and rural-urban counties was obtained for each state. Since there were only 72 metropolitan counties in the region, 15 of which were in Texas, all the metropolitan counties in 12 states were used, while a directed sample of the metropolitan counties of Texas was obtained by the method described. Through these procedures 161 counties in the region for these classifications were obtained.

Nine states of the 13 Southern states kept separate records in this period for the budget item of instruction according to race. Three rural counties of the sample did not report any expenditure for Negro schools and the expenditure records of one metropolitan county are incomplete. The number of counties used, therefore, in the analysis of expenditure in white and Negro schools at the county level are 33 in rural counties, 36 in rural-urban counties, and 40 in metropolitan counties. In order to be consistent among states, all districts included within counties selected, whether within separate city systems or in county systems, were aggregated to arrive at county statistics.

2. *Estimation of White and Negro Current Expenditures, 1951-52*

To estimate the white and Negro current expenditures for those states which do not report their data bi-racially, there are probably several methods available. The method used in this volume is as follows:

First, a multiple regression was computed. The dependent variable was total current expenditures—transportation not included—and the independent variables were white and Negro average daily attendance and a residual variable. The 1951-52 data were used for the thirteen states.

By means of the regression equation so derived cost breakdowns were computed. The weights of the parameters served to help particularly in the determination of the costs for the two races; they were applied along with the regression coefficients to assess that portion of total expenditures which could in all likelihood be allocated to each of the two races.

Second, these cost breakdowns, so estimated, were subjected to further scrutiny, governed by what was known about the spending practices of each state so that any exogenous factors caught by the residual variable could at least in part be accounted for.

Finally the data were checked over by various people who are in close touch with these kinds of data.

3. *How Long May It Take the South to Catch up with the North?*

From 1939-40 to 1949-50 the South increased its current expenditures on education markedly. The annual rate of 5.94 per cent exceeds significantly the average annual rate for the United States of 3.29 per cent. Should the South continue to spend at this rate it will catch up with the United States in its per pupil current expenditures by 1965.

The method of determining these rates and data is as follows.

The general formula for deriving the rates of expenditures may be stated: $E_{49-50} = E_{39-40} (1 + r)^{10}$, where E_{39-40} is the symbol for the expenditures in the fiscal year 1939-40 and E_{49-50}, those for 1949-50; "r" is the rate and it is made the unknown; and the power "10," the number of years in the decade. The solution of the equation is facilitated by the use of logarithms.

Write for the United States, using the deflated data:

$$\$121.48 = \$87.91 \, (1+r)^{10}$$
$$\log 121.48 - \log 87.91 = 10 \log (1+r)$$
$$2.0845048 - 1.9440383 = 10 \log (1+r)$$
$$\log (1+r) = .01404665$$
$$(1+r) = 1.03287$$
$$r = 3.29 \text{ per cent, the rate for U. S.}$$

Write for the South, using the deflated data:

$$\$83.26 = \$46.75 \, (1+r)^{10}$$
$$\log 83.26 - \log 46.75 = 10 \log (1+r)$$
$$1.9204364 - 1.6697816 = 10 \log (1+r)$$
$$\log (1+r) = .02506548$$
$$(1+r) = 1.05941$$
$$r = 5.94 \text{ per cent, the rate for the South.}$$

The annual rate in the South is nearly twice as great as that for the nation. The ratio is 1.8:1, reflecting the above percentage growth.

Should the South continue to expand its outlays at that rate—the evidence is that the 1954-55 rate is even greater—it should catch up with the nation in not too distant a future. In fact, by use of a simple technique this is found to be 1965. The method of determining the year of catching-up is as follows. Given the experience rates above, the Southern current expenditures per pupil in average daily attendance would equal the United States expenditures when: $\$83.26 \, (1.05941)^x = \$121.48 \, (1.03287)^x$, where the figures in the brackets are the antilogs of $1+r$ for the South and the United States respectively. The solution is:

$$\log 83.26 + x \log 1.05941 = \log 121.48 + x \log 1.03287$$
$$1.9204364 + x \, (0.02506548) = 2.0845048 + x \, (0.01404665)$$
$$0.01101883x = .1640684$$
$$x = 15 \text{ years, i.e., 1965}$$

On the assumption that economic trends will continue to be favorable, this expectation may be said to be fairly certain.

For those people who seek to have the South spending in 1960 as much as does the entire nation, the Southern rate must be increased by 1.32 per cent; according to this goal spending should be changing at an annual rate of 7.26 per cent. This rate is 2.21 times as great as the national rate for the 1940's decade and obviously would involve a stupendous effort.

In the derivation of these rates the Southern region and the United States have both been treated as units. Some Southern states are actually spending at a rate equal to or greater than that for the nation; others are spending at significantly lower rates.

4. *Methods for Projection of Enrollment*

There are three methods for the projection of enrollment. The first, the conversion of census population figures for each area into enrollment figures, is probably the most precise. It is preferred by demographers and population statisticians. Briefly put, it involves the listing for each area of the census figures by each school-age year and moving each year so obtained ahead into the next. Assuming no migration, the preceding year's enrollment for a given age would become the enrollment for the next year with subtraction for the number expected to die within the year. An actuarially determined death rate is obtained from the United States Mortality Table; this table is preferred because it does not leave out any population element. (The usual insurance mortality tables are based upon relatively select populations and therefore should not be applied.)

If migration is expected an adjustment would be made to include it, plus or minus, according to the expectations for the area.

The second method involves the projection of the enrollment experience by grades (or school ages) on the basis of the population for a series of school years—a series of at least five years and preferably more. A mathematical curve may be fitted to this "time series" of enrollment for a given grade by statistical methods (least squares or product moment). The curve so derived for the past period may be extended into the future by means of its formula.

This method is highly empirical, and its tenability rests on the assumption that what happened in the past will happen in the future. The results may not be as readily modified for deviations from experience as under the first method. The first method may give greater "internal consistency" because the projection is year by year and is based solely upon the past year's experience. The second method may, however, discover trends in population more readily than the first, and it takes cognizance of the death and migration experience simultaneously.

The third method, the method used in this study, goes out directly from the population estimates for each school-age year. Each year's census, age by age, is first corrected for the number of pupils who enter private and parochial schools. This number is based upon actual experience. Since most Southern children enter the public schools of the region, in many Southern states the necessary adjustment is relatively minor compared with the national averages.

Next, in the same table immediately below the school population census for the series of five or more years and for each age, the actual enrollment data are entered. Percentages of enrollment to the adjusted school-age population are then derived. These percentages may be averaged to give single "experience ratios" for each age group.

In this method, followed in principle in this study, the enrollments for the four age groups, 5-6, 7-13, 14-15, and 16-17, as given by the United States Census for the census year 1950 for the Southern states in total are divided by the corresponding populations of the four age groups. This division results in an unadjusted ratio of enrollment to population. These, converted into percentages, are derived for each state and for each age group. To eliminate that portion of the school-age population which attends private and parochial schools the unadjusted percentages for each state of the four groups are multiplied by another percentage which gives effect to that portion of the school-age population which attends public schools only.

A modification in method is now introduced. Rather than averaging the ratios as done above, a trend line is fitted to the ratios for the entire series of years by least square techniques. The trends so found may then be projected to yield the expected percentages which would be applied to the projected school-age population.

In this study, first an arbitrary set of ratios, based upon the experience of Oklahoma, Florida, and so on, is determined for each of the four age groups. A second set has been derived by the method of trend line projection. The arbitrary set of ratios compares so favorably with the mathematically determined ratios that no major adjustments seem necessary.

5. *Estimation of Capital Deficit*

The estimates of the capital deficit, to be sure, are crude. Nevertheless, concerted effort has been made to check state reports and other sources on questions related to depreciation and the age of buildings. Unfortunately, the data on the age of buildings are deficient, and the validation of the "write-off" is only partial.

There is another way of estimating the total "real" values of the existing plant and equipment considered adequate. The payments into insurance reserves are converted or capitalized into these values. An average fire rate for the state is computed by weighting the various rates related to kinds of building and protection. This average fire rate is then made into a multiplier, and this multiplier in turn is multiplied by the payments into the reserves. The result, after correction for decimals, is the total value of existing plant and equipment. Thus, no data on plant and equipment values were available for the State of Tennessee. An estimate of the present value was obtained by this method of capitalization. Insurance rates of $0.85 for county schools and of $0.12 for city schools are assumed. These figures in themselves are representative rather than actual. They are combined into a multiplier through two computations. First, they are averaged together by assigning weights of 70 to the county rate and 30 to the city rate. These weights are based upon the percentages that the county and city average daily attendance bear to the total. The average so obtained is then divided into 1; the quotient is the multiplier, 1.56. The payments for insurance in Tennessee amounted to approximately $625,000; this figure is the total amount of insurance premiums less estimated expenses. The product of multiplier and $625,000, with correction for decimals, is $98,000,000, the value of the existing plant and equipment. Even though this method has not been refined, it resulted in depreciated values not significantly different from those derived by the "write-off" method. Whether the problem of equalization in this area of expenditure has been wholly resolved is debatable. Obviously, as in the case of current expenditures, what is an equal expenditure for capital purposes is very difficult to convert into a truly meaningful statistical concept. There is some validity, however, in the assumption implicit in the analysis so that, by the above treatment of values and needed improvements, something like "identical facilities" may be had.

6. *Cost Factor for Determining Growth in Capital Requirements*

In Alabama the construction cost per square foot in 1951-52 dollars is $7.50. To derive the cost factor for Alabama this figure is multiplied first by the standard footage 45 to get the cost factor for the elementary schools; second, by 60 to get the cost factor for the secondary schools in that state. The same procedure is followed for all states; the variation in the cost factor comes from the regional differences in the cost per square foot. The cost factors for the elementary schools are then multiplied by the increment in elementary school enrollment state by state; and the cost factors for the secondary schools are multiplied by the increment in the secondary school enrollment. These products are next summed and multiplied by 1.0938 to give total capital and equipment costs for each state necessary to take care of the increased enrollment. This equipment cost factor is arbitrarily chosen, but it grows out of observation of practices in school administration. Finally, each of these totals is divided by 10 to give the needed yearly outlay in plant and equipment stated in terms of dollars.

To illustrate, Alabama by our assumptions may expect over the period, 1950-1960, increments of 142,000 in elementary schools and 57,000 in secondary schools. For the cost of elementary capital needs, 142,000 times the cost factor $337.50 ($7.50 x 45) gives the total by 1960, of $47,925,000. The total cost of plant for the secondary schools is 57,000 times $450 ($7.50 x 60) or $25,650,000. Sum $47,925,000 and $25,650,000 and multiply by 1.0938, to obtain total outlay for plant and equipment which should be made by the state of Alabama to meet the anticipated growth in enrollment through 1959-1960 from 1949-50, or $80,476,000. The multiplier, 1.0938, is the sum of 1 and 0.0938; 0.0938 is assumed to be the ratio of equipment to plant value.

To get the annual outlay in capital and equipment requirement, we simply divide $80,476,000 by 10. For Alabama it is $8,047,600. Knowing the value of capital and equipment in 1951-52, this annual outlay obviously may be accumulated to get the total value that the plant and equipment would have in 1960, on the assumption of no depreciation. The taking of depreciation by public authority in educational plant and equipment seems unnecessary, because there is no problem of pricing. Buildings are replaced when no longer fit for use (and there is no general acceptable concept of fitness in defining depreciation).

7. *An Analysis of the Costs of Integration*

Actually, in the light of the limited experience with integration, the question of whether integration will effect economies or will increase costs is quite unsettled.

Savings conceivably may be effected in certain cases; where white schools now are not fully utilized, occupancy of a building by both races could eliminate the cost of a new building for the purpose of housing Negroes in the vicinity. These conditions of unused capacity develop under the change in the racial composition of the population where urbanization of a city or area is on the rise. But for the most part, the school population is growing at such a pace that the actual problem is the converse: insufficient space for either race.[1]

Expenditures on public schools are very closely geared to the number of pupils; current expenditures, to the ADA; and the capital expenditures, to enrollment. This proposition is borne out in part by statistical evidence.

In other words, school expense, current and capital, tend to vary directly with the variations in the number of pupils. Those educational costs which do not vary to any degree are relatively minor; therefore, savings through integration would also seem to be relatively minor. Moreover, those instances in which savings could be effected are scattered, and it would be almost impossible to take them into consideration in our estimation of the reduction

1. Ernst W. Swanson, "Some Economic Effects of the Supreme Court Decision," *Journal of Public Law*, Vol. 3, No. 1, p. 126.

in costs which could come were integration accomplished. No adjustment for such possible reductions is thus made here.

On the other hand, there are school districts or counties in which integration might even force an increase in expenditures. For example, in order to bring about better working relationships between the two races in the educational program, additional administrative and supervisory staff may be necessary. In fact, the frictions of adjustment may require somewhat different approaches to education particularly as problems in group behavior develop. Much time may have to be spent on the part of all associated with the schools in the study of and research into methods of group control. Integration, if and when it comes, is not going to be cost free.

In net, the savings in some cases may be offset by the higher costs incurred in others.[2]

Correlation of capital outlays and enrollment has not been attempted here. These expenditures are made too irregularly and only a time series of a dozen or so years would have yielded the proper correlation; such data were not made available.

But the correlations of current expenditures with ADA definitely support the proposition. The findings are: (a) the multiple correlation coefficient for the regression of current expenditures on white ADA and Negro ADA, for the year 1951-52 for the thirteen states, is 0.95, or 0.05 short of being perfect. The ADA by the breakdown between the two races thus accounts for over 90 per cent of the variability in expenditures; (b) the simple correlation coefficient for the regression of current expenditures for the same year and group of states on the total ADA, or no breakdown between races, is 0.94. Again, around 90 per cent of the variability is accounted for by ADA.

In net, such results clearly indicate that there is but one significant factor determining the variations in current expenditures, ADA.

8. *Methods of Income Projection*

Methods of national and regional income projections have been greatly improved over the last two decades. This improvement has been accompanied by a marked advance in the collection of basic income statistics through the research efforts of the National Bureau of Economic Research and the Department of Commerce. Consequently income forecasting has been more and more successful; to be sure, it is still subject to fairly sizable errors.

The most recent methods are quite elaborate and involve applications of economic models which employ numerous intricate variables.[3]

2. *Ibid.*, pp. 126-27.
3. The most impressive have been those based upon what the economist-statistician terms "aggregative models." These models often incorporate a large number of variables to reflect or determine the changes in incomes. For example, the expenditures of households and business firms and their savings are the

This elaborateness virtually prohibits their use in the projections undertaken in this study. Certain kinds of data which must be injected into the models cannot be had on any long-run basis without introducing too much room for error. Moreover, the number of variables which must also be predicted increase. For present purposes, models that are relatively simple in construction are employed. While certain students of model building may be critical of their simplicity, once the nature of their limitations is understood income may be projected over a span of years with some validity.

In the study two models are employed. The first is based on the fairly conservative assumption that once the effects of the war years are eliminated, income growth in the South year after year is at a fairly constant amount somewhat governed by the pre-war experience. The growth in income is considered to be linear or straight-line, as in the case of a simple series of numbers, 2, 4, 6, 8, and 10. The trend or line of growth is usually found by the application of statistical techniques. The generalized formula applied in this instance is given by the equation: $Y = A + Bt$, where "Y" is the trend value of income to be found; "A," the trend value at the middle year of the series of data being analyzed; "B," the slope or the year-by-year changes in income; and "t," the year. (See F. E. Croxton and D. J. Cowden, *Applied General Statistics*, Ch. 15.) Furthermore, the growth rate is assumed to be relatively low.

The second model is based on the proposition that the income growth approaches a geometric curve, a reflection largely of the post-war developments. Thus, the series of numbers, 2, 4, 8, 16, 32, and 64 represents a simplified case. The trend or line of growth may be found by statistical techniques or by the more simple application of the compound interest formula.

The linear or straight-line model will produce income values for the coming years which will lie below the values to be had by the geometric model. This second model is particularly characterized by an increasing rate of growth.

The assumption really underlying the first model is that the expansion of the Southern economy under industrialization, while for

reflection of their decisions in the use of past and present income (and frequently borrowings); and, in turn, these variables tend to determine the future behavior of the total or aggregate income of the economy.

For those readers well trained in mathematics and statistics, the following volume is recommended as an introduction to the study of income projection: Lawrence R. Klein, *A Textbook of Econometrics* (Evanston, Ill.: Row, Peterson and Company, 1953). For less technical treatments these are recommended: Elmer C. Bratt, *Business Cycles and Forecasting* (Homewood, Ill.: Richard D. Irwin, Inc., 1953) and Frank D. Newberry, *Business Forecasting* (New York: McGraw-Hill Book Co., New York, 1952).

the time-being rapid, will shortly take on a steady, even, year-by-year development through the remainder of the decade. Such an assumption places the future pattern of growth on a relatively conservative path. The Southern economy would therefore tend to follow closely the pattern set by the national economy since the 1880's.

To be sure, should unexpected changes occur there may be deviations from the projections so derived. The discovery of important new resources, the location of a new large industry, the shifting of sizable governmental operations, and so on may each cause a displacement of the trend. As such developments occur, some adjustment must be made in the projections. But the argument usually offered is that these deviations are not in themselves powerful enough to throw off general growth significantly.

The assumption underlying the application of the second or the geometric model is that the Southern economy is still in the formative stages of industrialization. Therefore, the rate of growth for some time to come will be at an increasingly upward rate. As industrialization is more and more intensified the growth in income will also be intensified. The probability of this happening is particularly high since the region up until the time of its metamorphosis had been devoted largely to farming on a fairly primitive scale. With the change, the rate of increase in income is not only accelerated, but the growth at such rates may extend into several decades, dependent upon the nature and degree of industrialization. If farming is more and more converted into modern agriculture with its own form of industrialization, the developments could be especially pronounced. In the South there is increasing evidence that this is the nature of the pattern of growth. (See Calvin B. Hoover and B. U. Ratchford, *Economic Resources and Policies of the South*, New York, Macmillan Company, 1951.)

9. *Estimation of the "Low" Income*

The first model provides the "low" limit of the range and the second model, the "high" limit. Such projections do not incorporate any estimates on what the cyclical changes in income will be; the assumption is that such fluctuations will be at a minimum.

In computing the "low" series, before the trend lines are found, the data on income are adjusted for price level changes. The Bureau of Labor Statistics Consumers' Price Index with the base 1935-1939 has been used. Once the trend values are determined they will be blown up to the price level existing for each given year. The correction for the price-level fluctuations in the first place is of course for the purpose of eliminating the inflationary and deflationary effects of our national monetary and fiscal actions. Moreover, a line fitted to deflated data will in all likelihood produce a better measure of growth than would trend lines fitted to current dollar data. The effects of the war period are thus largely eliminated.

To determine properly the growth in any time series such as income payments, it is necessary to find trend lines for a period longer than the longest business cycle experienced during the period investigated. The fifteen years of income chosen here should give a desirable duration; it more than covers the post-war cycle lasting into 1949-50. The year 1938 is chosen as the beginning year for such series for a very simple reason: since 1952 is not a peak year but is adjacent to a peak year, 1953, which is the top of the second post-war cycle, then the beginning year should have the same characteristic. It happens that 1938 is adjacent to a peak year, 1937, the nearest high-income point falling towards the beginning of the period. The choice of the wrong beginning year may give a wrong trend.

The actual total income payments for the South rise from $11.1 billions in 1938 to $51.0 billions in 1952. To measure this trend, these data are first corrected for price level changes to give the deflated (or "real") income. The trend line is then fitted to these data. The annual growth or trend value is $1,070,000,000. This value is added accumulatively for fourteen years, beginning with the 1938 value, $13 billions, to give the final trend figure in 1952 of $28 billions of total income payments.

Total income payments may now be projected into 1960. The simplest way is to extend the deflated trend values through 1960 by the cumulative addition of the annual growth factor of $1,070,000,000. Thus, the expected deflated income for the South for 1960 in terms of the average prices for 1935-1939, the base period of the Bureau of Labor Statistics Consumers' Price Index, is $36.6 billions. The increase from 1952 through 1960 is $8.6 billions.

These projected year-by-year figures are next converted into 1952 prices. Each yearly value is multiplied by 189.7, the price index number for 1952. Now all the projected values are stated in 1952 dollars, and analysis in terms of a constant dollar is thus made possible. Total income payments for the South so stated are expected to reach $67.3 billions in 1960. See Table 64; the low income row for the South shows these final figures.

In the later examination of ability to pay in the Southern states, total income payments projections for each state will be required. The same trend computation as applied to the data for the whole South is applied to the data by states for the period 1938 through 1952. Then projections are made in the manner just described, but, of course, for the state data.

10. *Estimation of the "High" Income*

If the chances are fairly good that the Southern economy will enjoy an increasing rate of intensity of industrialization then, obviously, future income should rise in accordance with that rate. In turn, this rate should be amplified by the increasing rate of growth of population. Hence, in the method for projecting the high income departs in two respects from the previous method.

First, only per capita income data will be analyzed and projected. Second, because of the rate of change that is anticipated, a curve of growth which corresponds with the rate of change must be found. The compound interest formula which perhaps gives effect to growth the best of any of the possible curves is therefore applied. Although it could be used, the previous method of fitting trend lines by statistical techniques is now abandoned. The present technique should prove less complicated.

There are two steps to this approach. The first involves the determination of the annual rate of growth of per capita income for the region and the states over the years 1938-1952. Naturally, the income data are corrected for price level changes. Again, the Bureau of Labor Statistics Consumers' Price Index is used for the purpose.

The application of the compound interest formula to this determination of what the trend has been, 1938 through 1952, gives the annual rates of growth stated as percentages. For the thirteen states these rates are: Alabama, 6.15; Arkansas, 5.59; Florida, 3.75; Georgia, 5.64; Kentucky, 5.54; Louisiana, 4.62; Mississippi, 6.27; North Carolina, 4.80; Oklahoma, 5.41; South Carolina, 6.52; Tennessee, 5.57; Texas, 5.05; and Virginia, 4.49.

That these rates will hold through the 1950's is assumed. This assumption is in line with the earlier proposition on the possible increasing intensity of industrialization.

The second step necessitates the inversion of the compound interest formula. In the first instance the rates of growth were determined. Now, having found these, how much dollar income will grow during the remainder of the decade is estimated on the argument that it will rise for each state at the rate experienced in that state. The required formula is: $Y_t = Y_o (1 + r)^t$, where Y_t is the value to which the base year income, Y_o, will grow over "t" years, given the interest rate "r." To apply this formula we invert it so that "r" is made the "unknown," i.e., the value for which we solve, and Y_t and Y_o are given.

First the rate of growth per year over the period 1938-1952 is determined. The values for Y_t and Y_o are substituted into the formula; then the rate "r," with "t" made equal to 14, is found.

The solution is best done by the use of logarithms and the formula is written:

(2) $\qquad \log (1 + r) = (\log Y_t - \log Y_o)/t,$

where "r" is the unknown.

The next step is to project the growth so found into the year desired; say 1960. This may be done by inverting formula (2) as follows:

$$\log Y_t = \log Y_b + t \log (1 + r).$$

The unknown is now $\log Y_t$, the expected value for 1960; $\log Y_b$ is the base year from which the projection is made; in this case, 1952.

The actual computations for the two steps, using Alabama data, are

Step 1: $\quad \log (1 + r) = (\log Y_{1952} - \log Y_{1938})/t$
$= (2.72673 - 2.36361)/14$
$= .025937$
Antilog $(1 + r) = .106154$
$r = 6.15$ per cent

Step 2: $\quad \log Y_{1960} = Y_{1952} + 8 \log (1 + .0615)$
$= 2.72673 + 8 \; (.025937)$
$= 2.93423$
Antilog $= \$859.$

The deflated per capita income, for example, for Alabama in 1938 is $231. By 1952, this amount had grown to $533. This increase represents an annual rate of growth of 6.15 per cent. The $533 is now permitted to grow over the years 1952 to 1960 at this rate. The per capita income for Alabama in 1960 is therefore expected to be $859. By multiplying this figure by the price index number for 1952, 189.7, this amount may be reflated into 1952 dollars, or $1630. Thus Alabama's per capita income in 1952 is $1,012. Setting aside effects from inflation it will increase by $618 through the rest of the 1950's.

The per capita projections are of course converted into total income payments by multiplying the given-year per capita income for each state by the expected population for each state.

www.ingramcontent.com/pod-product-compliance
Lightning Source LLC
Chambersburg PA
CBHW030115010526
44116CB00005B/256